Dedication for 1st Printing

This book is dedicated to all cowboy poets, folk singers and reciters, young and old.

Mason Coggin

Janice Coggin

Dedication for 2nd Printing

In loving memory of Janice and Mason Coggin, who installed in me a great passion for rhymes, histories and mysteries of the West.

Diane Coggin [illegible]

Contents

Forward

There is one cowboy poet whose work has the absolute, real, bona fide, gritty ring of experience and truth. Bruce Kiskaddon lived the life. He wrangled, he roped, he rode, he wrecked, he suffered all kinds of weather. He did not embellish the life. The meter is less than technically perfect. But he remembers and re-creates the historic world of the ranch and range of the late 19th and early 20th century. His words echo the ones heard on the frontier.

From the nearly 400 pieces that he did, Janice and Mason Coggin have selected the best. They have included many of the drawings of Katherine Field who illustrated much of his work after the mid 30s. From the stories about critters from bedbugs to the biggest animals, his poetry begs to be recited. From lonely cowboy herder and the isolated line shacks to the community celebrations of Christmas, we hear the early west in an authoritative voice.

Janice and Mason used many sources for Bruce Kiskaddon poems. They selected from *Rhymes of the Ranges* published in 1924, *Western Poems* published 1935, and, *Rhymes of the Ranges and Other Poems* published in 1947. Janice always chose the earliest sources for the collection.

Larry Maurice has aided them immeasurably by providing a number of poems from magazines and calendars published by the Los Angeles Union Stockyards and the Western Livestock Journal including the poems which Bruce wrote as "The Holaday & Hampton Poet." They researched the libraries in Arizona. Often they had several sources, if not versions, for the same poem. They also found that Bruce had sometimes written more than one poem with the same name.

The Coggins have collected and published the finest book of Kiskaddon poems. As a Kiskaddon enthusiast, I can only hope that Janice and Mason will find more unpublished poems, combine them with the existing poems, and publish a second volume.

John Shaver, Co-Chair Cochise
Cowboy Poetry and Music Gathering

Acknowledgments

To Tom and Nancy Luce and Vi Wosilait, owners of the old Y-Lightening Ranch near Sierra Vista, Arizona, a big thank you for a copy of their 1935 book, Western Poems by Kiskaddon, which started us on the trail of other Kiskaddon poems and resulted in this book.

One of the hardest jobs we had was the selection of the poems for this book. Thanks to John Shaver of Sierra Vista, AZ, the co-ramrod of the Cochise County Cowboy Gathering, for the following: a copy of the collection of Kiskaddon poems that he had collected, his help in writing the foreword and in the choice of these poems.

To Larry Maurie a thank you for providing photocopies of calendars and magazines containing Kiskaddon poems and for providing information about the pseudonym "Holaday and Hampton Poet."

A special thanks to Tom Sharpe of Grand Junction, CO, a cowboy well known by those who gather for cowboy poetry, for a copy of his collection, facts about Kiskaddon's life and his unfailing help.

Hal Cannon of the Western Folklife Center in Elko edited a book of Kiskaddon poems in 1987. His excellent description of Kiskaddon's life and poems gave us a deeper insight into the poetry and songs.

Sue Wallis of the Western Folklife Center has been most helpful and encouraging.

Thanks to Roger Meyer of the Special Collections at the University of Arizona Library in Tucson and to Michael Wurtz of the Sharlot Hall Museum library in Prescott Arizona, for finding and copying the Kiskaddon poetry in their collections.

The following poem was written as in introduction to *Rhymes of the Ranges* published in 1924 by Bruce Kiskaddon.

Introductory

These are just a few rhymes of old friends and old times,
And I hope before I am through –
Just once in a while they will bring a broad smile,
To the face of some old buckaroo.

Wherever he worked in the days that are past,
On the mountain, the plain or the valley,
What matters it now if he tied hard and fast
Or tumbled his steer with a dally.

If he wrangled the bunch, if he rode gentle strings,
If he topped off the wild ones that shimmy –
If he rode with his leathers through centre fire rings,
Or sat on a double-rigged rimmy.

If he worked for big outfits far out on the plains,
Where they never had use for a packer,
Or back in the hills in the snow and the rains,
With the regular old greasy sacker.

If he worked as a drifter and trusted to luck,
If he managed a bunch of his own;
If he cooked at the wagon and put up the chuck,
Or held down a line camp alone.

They are plain simple tales, of the round-ups and trails,
When he worked on the range with the cattle;
Not of wild woolly nights, nor of gambling hall fights,
But the days and the nights in the saddle.

Introduction

Bruce Kiskaddon, born in Pennsylvania in 1878, began his ranch life in 1898 in the district called Picket Wire, cowboy pronunciation of Purgatory where the Purgatory River runs in southern Colorado. Several poems reflect the thoughts, ideas and experiences of a youngster on the range, such as "Your First Saddle" and "Your First Trip." "The Trinidad Boy," not included in this book, is set in Colorado.

In *Rhymes of the Ranges and Other Poems* published in 1947 Kiskaddon writes of his work on "Tap" Duncan's ranch, the Diamond Bar in Mohave County, Arizona, and the encouragement he received from Duncan to put his songs, verses and jingles into writing. "Tap," an old time Texas and Arizona rancher, is featured in "Our Boss." The Diamond Bar name and the semi-arid countryside of west central Arizona appear in many of Kiskaddon's poems.

Kiskaddon served in the First World War in France with the cavalry where he added to his knowledge of "The Troop Hoss." He was a buckaroo in Australia for a time before returning to Arizona.

In the late 1920s, Kiskaddon went to Hollywood to wrangle horses and play bit parts in the movies, but found that it was easier and more lucrative to work as a bellhop in the hotels. Several of his poems relating to hotel life are found in his book, *Just As Is*, published in 1928.

For the rest of his life he wrote and consolidated his poetry. In 1935, he published a book called *Western Poems,* which also featured Katherine Field's illustrations. Katherine Field was born and raised on a ranch in central New Mexico. Even though they never met, through their correspondence her illustrations became an important part of many of his poems.

Although several of his poems have been sung, only a few were found that actually had choruses. Two in this book are "Cowboys Pants" and "The Graves by the Side of the Road." Several, such as "Hoof Beats" have been put to music.

The Los Angles Union Stockyards featured his poems and illustrations in calendars from 1939 through 1959. His work, accompanied by the illustrations was also published in the Western Livestock Journal. The poems became cherished collectors items by westerners and found their way into many old scrapbooks.

This book features 108 poems of almost 400 written and published by Kiskaddon. Poems from the 1924 publication are in the original form. All unusual spelling and creative punctuation are Kiskaddon originals.

Mason and Janice Coggin

KatherineField

Alone

The hills git awful quiet,
when you have to camp alone.
It's mighty apt to set a feller thinkin'.
You always half way waken
when a hoss shoe hits a stone,
Or you hear the sound
of hobble chains a clinkin'.

It is then you know the idees
that you really have in mind.
You think about the things
you've done and said.
And you sometimes change
the records that you nearly always find
In the back of almost
every cow boy's head.

It gives a man a soter
different feelin' in his heart.
And he sometimes gits
a little touch of shame,
When he minds the times and places
that he didn't act so smart,
And he knows himself
he played a sorry game.

It kinda makes you see yourself
through other people's eyes.
And mebby so yore pride
gits quite a fall.
When yore all alone and thinkin',
well, you come to realize
Yo're a mighty common feller after all.

An Experiment

I'm jest a old, hard and fast "rimmy"
That's allus worked one certain way,
I was talkin' to Eddie and Jimmie –
And it's better to dally, they say.
Now you often have heard people talkin'
That it don't hurt a feller to try
I never was much hand fer knockin',
But I'm willin' to state that's a lie.

It was on the beef hunt last September
I jumped a big three-year-old steer
He gave me a few to remember,
He went through the brush like a deer.
He certainly knowed how to do it.
He was leavin' from there like a bat.
But I sez, "Jest you help yourself to it,
I'll soon be around where you're at.

The hoss I was ridin', I'm sayin,
Was lazy but not very slow.
He had the world cheated fer stayin',
If you'd spur him ,you bet he could go.
That steer? Hadn't no chance to turn him-
He wasn't the turn around breed
So I reckoned I'd start in and learn him
By breakin' the critter to lead.

I sent my old loop his direction,
I jerked it and let the rope cross,
Then I aimed for to make a connection
Betwixt that said steer and my hoss.
I dabbed fer my winds on "Old Sally,"
But the hoss sort of shirked and hung back.
I thought I had room fer a daily
But the steer got away with my slack.

Then my whole constitution jest buckles –
Like when somebody tromps on your –
Fer the end of my rope and my knuckles,
Was all that I got on the horn.
My hand was all busted and mangled.
Got one crooked finger now. See?
Well, I follered the steer till he tangled,
And got him tied up to a tree.

There is certain sad memories that lingers,
And I reckon that this one will last.
It may be my neck, not my fingers,
But I'll risk it and tie hard and fast

(Borein)

Ants In His Pants

From the way this here old cow boy
    is takin' off his pants,
It would seem he's got acquainted
    with a nest of big red ants.
And his hoss is shore oneasy,
    with his eyes and nostrils wide;
Fer he thinks that human bein'
    is takin' off it's hide.

Some folks say the red ants string you
    and some others say they bite.
Once they start a workin' on you,
    you will swear they both are right.
Fer the pain they give will chill you
    and it ain't a bit of fun
What they do is shore a plenty,
    makes no difference how it's done.

You can see the wind's a blowin'
    he's about to lose his hat.
And it makes his shirt tail flutter
    as it sweeps across the flat.
And the hoss? It ain't no wonder
    that he starts to jump and snort.
He is just a half broke pony
    workin' on a hackamore.

He caint make out what has happened,
    and he wouldn't onderstand,
If the cow boy chased his hat
    and packed his "Levis" in his hand.
When you've got a half broke broncho,
    there's a mighty healthy chance
That most any thing can happen
    if the ants git in yore pants.

Alkali Ike's Zippers

"Now speakin' of Zippers," sez Alkali Ike,
"Them zippers is sumpthin' I really don't like.
I aimed to buy clothes like I always had wore,
Till I started a lookin' around in the store.

They had some new shirts and some new overalls.
That fastened with zippers, no buttons aytall.
I reckoned that clothes with a riggin' like that
Would be fine fer the boys on the Alkali Flat.

Because where there's alkali water to drink,
Things may happen sooner than what you might think.
So I got me some clothes that was rigged up like that,
And went back to my camp on the Alkali Flat.

Next mornin' I'd traveled fer mebby a mile,
When the time come to give them new zippers a trial.
I grabbed at the handle and give 'em a jerk
But holey old golden them zippers don't work.

I swear and I swear, I am shore out of luck.
I have started 'em crooked, the zipper is stuck.
I fuss and I pull till I git the thing straight,
Then the zipper it works, but a little too late.

The next thing I do is to throw them new garments
Up onto a cactus fer ants and fer varmints.
And I reckon that buttons is safer at that,
Fer fellers that lives on the Alkali Flat.

All Dressed Up

Things is pickin' up as most folks knows,
So I sent to town fer to git new clo'es.
Some onderwear and a big hat box,
A couple of shirts and a passel of socks.

Some overalls and other truck,
Three red bandannys throwed in fer luck,
My boots aint new but they'll do right well,
I reckon I'll make them last a spell.

I'll be the pride of the whole derned spread
With a fust class Stetson on my head.
A bran new slicker tied on behind—
It's strange how yore clo'es improves yore mind.

Nice new clo'es purtects the hide
And sorter contents a man inside.
Clo'es does a heap toward makin' the man.
Try gain' without and you'll onderstand.

The Balky Hoss

The pleasant recollections is the ones
  that mostly last,
But there's sometimes other memories
  come a creepin' from the past.
How you lost your summer's wages,
  on a horse you thought could run.
How a big buck stood and watched
  you when you didn't have a gun.
Then one evening at a shindig,
  you thought you was doin' fine
Till some people come and told you
  you was gittin' out of line.
You rode ten miles to a dance once.
  When you got there you was sore.
You had got your dates all tangled.
  It had been the night before.

You have got some recollections
  of some gal that let you down,
But remember when your hoss balked
  on the main street right in town.
Yes, you had a sneaky feelin'
  that you mebby wasn't boss
When he turned around and throwed
  his head across the other hoss.
You would like to took a rifle and
  have downed him with some slugs.
He was lookin' at you pig eyed
  standin' crosswise in the tugs.
You hated the old critter
  till you wisht that he was dead.
You would like to took a hammer
  and just knocked him in the head.

Then the crowd all gathered round
    you fer to git in on the show.
Every one of them could tell you
    what to do to make him go.
There was some that said he'd ort
    to be jest tickled with a switch.
Some said beat him with a stay chain,
    others said to git a twitch.
Some said to git a jocky stick
    and that would help perhaps
While others said to put one ear
    inside the head stall straps.
Some said punch him in the belly.
    Others said pick up his feet.
And one allowed he ort to
    have a little bite to eat.

The tough guys said to choke him
    and to shut off all his wind.
Or mebbyso to knock him down
    and let him up ag'in.
One said that he could start him
    with some paper and a match.
Or put a rope behind his knees
    and saw to make him stretch.
Oh yes, there was a hundred things
    they wanted you to try.
One was to take tobacker juice
    and squirt it in his eye.
You tried to keep your temper.
    You was shakin', you was pale.
Every now and then some wise guy
    asked you if he was fer sale.

But it wasn't no use tryin'
    and your temper got plum lost
When some feller on the side walk
    yelled and asked how much he cost.
And when you got to hatin'
    every body in your heart,
The hoss got tired waitin',
    straightened out and made a start.
It surely was a big relief
    to git out on the road.
Got some cuss words off your stummick;
    eased your mind quite a load.
You swore to God you'd never drive
    that hoss to town ag'in.
You swapped him to another man.
    You thought he didn't know.
But he hadn't any trouble gittin'
    that old hoss to go.
It sort of set you thinkin'
    and the idee come to you,
That there might be balky hosses,
    but there's balky drivers too.

Between the Lines

There's something I'm not forgetting,
But it's something I could not say.
I could not arrange the setting
And the scene, in the proper way.
The air of the desert and mountain,
The smoke of the far out camp;
The whispering voice of the night wind
And the picketed horse's tramp;
The tread of the moving cattle,
The song that the riders croon,
The swing and the sway of the saddle
That goes to the lilt of the tune.

The race after wild young horses,
That beats any hunt for game;
And battle of wits and forces
Until the wild brutes are tame.
For the strong young steeds are fighters,
That are raised on the hills and plains;
They must learn to balance their riders—
You must teach them to answer the reins.
It calls for your skillful riders—
Your hardiest, strongest men.
The buck and bawl, the sickening fall,
And the whirl of the broncho pen.

The rush of the summer,
When the work is rough and hard
Beyond all understanding,
And the shivering nights on guard;
The quiet night in the summer,
When the air is damp and warm;
You hear the rumbling thunder
And watch the approaching storm.
When the heavens pour like a funnel,
And the Devil his own can claim;

When the sky is black as a tunnel,
Then white, with the lightening's flame!
It is then that the weak go under—
It calls for a hardy breed;
The shattering crash of the thunder,
And the rush of the mad stampede.

The terrible grip of the blizzard,
When the horse and rider reel;
The curse of the snow blind puncher,
And the frost bites that throb and peel.
The nights you hate to remember
Out in the line camp alone
When the gray wolves howled in the timber,
And the perishing cattle moaned.
You tried to keep track of the slaughter,
But the frost and the storm were king;
How you chopped the ice from the water
And prayed for an early spring.

Or down in the desert regions,
And the ranges far to the south,
Where the cattle swarm in legions,
And the stock man is caught in the drouth;
Springs are steadily failing—
Almost no place to go.
Coyotes are always wailing,
Buzzards are circling low.
What once were strong young cattle,
Are only suffering wrecks—
So thin that they seem to rattle
When you stick your knife in their necks.
Cattle too weak to gather—
You must try it although you fail;
Holding them up in the "Prather,"
"Chousing" them over the trail—

On every side they are crying,
"Take your cattle away;
Half of our own are drying–
No grass and water for strays."

Cow-boys in clothing tattered,
Faces and hands brush scarred;
Saddles and chaps all battered,
Horses look gaunt and hard.
The heat and the dust that smothers;
The tired out horse that lags;
The calves that have lost their mothers,
Wailing along in the drags.

That's why I'm giving you warning–
There's something I could not tell.
The joys as clear as the morning–
The tortures akin to Hell.
They never will reach outsiders,
Who were raised in the town's confines;
But they're here for the hard old riders,
Who can read them between the lines.

Bill The Snake Charmer

We never knowed the reason why,
But any thing Bill saw he'd try.
A circus was his last mistake,
He saw the man that charmed the snake.

As Bill was on his homeward road
With quite an alcoholic load,
A rattle snake beside the trail,
Stuck up his head and shuck his tail.

Pore Bill allowed he had a brake,
He got right down to charm the snake.
He sung a high and mornful whine
And tried to make the magic sign.

Bill's voice was high and over ripe
And rotten like a Hindoo pipe.
And Bill he sung like this. Sez he,
"Twee dee del dee! Twee dee del dee!"

Bill raised his hands above his head
And fetched 'em down with fingers spread
Right then pore Bill was out of luck
The rattle snake hauled off and struck.

Pore Bill had made his last wild ride.
His soul went shootin' down the slide.
An as he passed away, sez he,
"Twee dee del dee! Twee dee del dee!".

The Broncho Twister's Prayer*

It was a little grave yard
    on the rolling foot hill plains:
That was bleached by the sun in summer,
    swept by winter's snows and rains;
There a little bunch of settlers
    gathered on an autumn day
'Round a home made lumber coffin,
    with their last respects to pay.

Weary men that wrung their living
    from that hard and arid land,
And beside them stood their women;
    faded wives with toil worn hands.
But among us stood one figure
    that was wiry, straight and trim.
Every one among us know him.
    'Twas the broncho twister, Jim.

Just a bunch of hardened muscle
    tempered with a savage grit,
And he had the reputation
    of a man that never quit.
He had helped to build the coffin,
    he had helped to dig the grave;
And his instinct seemed to teach him
    how he really should behave.

Well, we didn't have a preacher,
    and the crowd was mighty slim.
Just two women with weak voices
    sang an old time funeral hymn.
That was all we had for service.
The old wife was sobbing there.
For her husband of a life time,
    laid away without prayer.

---

* Poem recited at Bruce Kiskaddon's funeral.

She looked at the broncho twister,
then she walked right up to him.
Put one trembling arm around him and said,
"Pray,. Please won't you Jim?"
You could see his figure straighten,
and a look of quick surprise
Flashed across his swarthy features,
and his hard dare devil eyes.

He could handle any broncho,
and he never dodged a fight.
'Twas the first time any body ever saw
his face turn white.
But he took his big sombrero
off his rough and shaggy head,
How I wish I could remember what
that broncho peeler said.

No, he wasn't educated.
On the range his youth was spent.
But the maker of creation
knew exactly what he meant.
He looked over toward the mountains
where the driftin' shadows played.
Silence must have reined in heaven
when they heard the way Jim prayed.

Years have passed since that small funeral
in that lonely grave yard lot.
But it gave us all a memory, and a lot
of food for thought.
As we stood beside the coffin,
and the freshly broken sod,
With that reckless broncho breaker
talkin' heart to heart with God.

When the prayer at last was over,
    and the grave had all been filled,
On his rough, half broken pony,
    he rode off toward the hills.
Yes, we stood there in amazement
    as we watched him ride away,
For no words could ever thank him.
    There was nothing we could say.
Since we gathered in that grave yard,
    it's been nearly fifty years.
With their joys and with their sorrows,
    with their hopes and with their fears.
But I hope when I have finished,
    and they lay me with the dead,
Some one says a prayer above me.
    like that broncho twister said.

The Buckboard

We read about the stage coach
and the covered wagon too;
And about the family surry
when we bought it shinin' new;
We hear about the bob sled
and about the one hoss sleigh,
But I'm telling you the buckboard
shore was handy in it's day.

The bed was on the axles, bolted
down between the wheels;
It was jest a row of wooden slats
but they was strong as steel.
An iron brace to rest your feet;
a rail around the top,
And a mighty handy foot brake
that would bring it to a stop.

It was built to travel distance
on a rough and rugged road;
They had cut off every pound they could
to lighten up the load.
The only springs it carried
was in onderneath the seat;
For a sturdy little wagon
it was mighty hard to beat.

I know the hoss and buggy days
have long since gone and past;
We travel in a motor car;
it's easy and it's fast.
But sometimes I git to wishin',
as strange as it may seem,
For an old slat bottomed buckboard
and a little knot-head team.

The Buggy Shack

Did you ever chance to waken in
the middle of the night?
And you couldn't be mistaken
it was shore a bed bug bight.
Part of them had started feedin'
and the rest was walkin' 'round,
What them varmints wasn't eatin'
they was really trompin' down.

Well, you found a couple matches
and you got the wall lamp lit.
By the time you got it lighted
they had all hid out and quit.
Then you stood outside the door way
fer to git a breath of air,
But you soon got mighty chilly,
posin' in yore onderwear.

So you got back into yore blankets
fer to git a little sleep,
But the way them bugs took to you
was enough to make you weep.
Bed bugs is as bad as grizzlies,
so I've often heard it said.
Grizzlies kill you, but them bed bugs
make you wish that you was dead.

You was cussin' and a-swearin'
you was mad enough to fight.
You could only put your clothes on
and set by the stove all night.
Fer you knowed they'd done and got you
when they made that sneak attack,
And yo're nothin' but a victim
when the bed bugs take the shack..

Bulls and Bears

There's a whole lot of space in that country out there,
So there art to be room for a bull and a bear.
But the bear he's a lookin' for sumphin' to eat,
And that long horned bull reckons he's after calf meat.

He thinks there ain't room for the two of them there,
So he figgers on doin' away with the bear.
A fightin' old bull seldom changes his mind.
He is out there protectin' his range and his kind.

Old long horn, I'd shore like to land on the scene
And cut into that fight with a heavy carbeen.
I'd go in on your side if it wasn't quite fair
And between me and you we'd shore waller that bear.

No, you wouldn't thank me, for when it was done,
I would have to take out with my hoss on the run.
You're a thankless old cuss, but then I wouldn't care.
You're protectin' your rights and you're doin' your share.

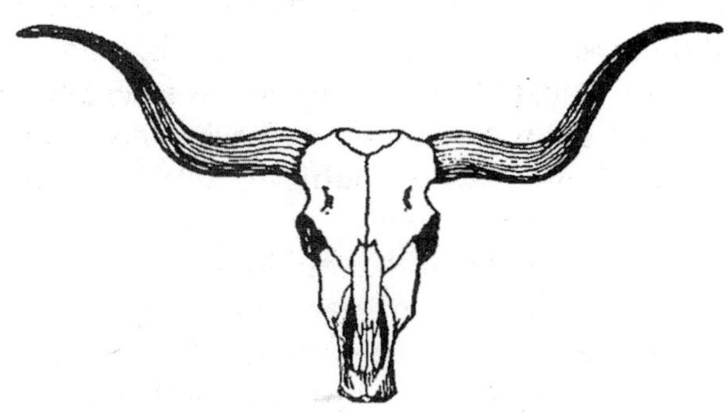

The Bunk House Mirror

That old bunk house mirror that most of us knew.
I remember it yet, and I know that you do.
One corner broke out, and a sort of a crack
That run half way across and a quarter way back.
The cheap wooden frame with the varnish all gone,
But the grease and the dirt and the fly specks stayed on.

And then the quicksilver was missin' in spots,
But that didn't bother a cow hand a lot.
He picked the good places and managed to shave
As he looked at his face in the ripples and wave.
No wonder the mirror was terribly wrecked
When you thought of the faces it had to reflect.

I know as a mirror it wasn't much class.
At its best it was only a cheap lookin' glass.
The old cord that held it was frayed quite a lot.
You could see where it broke and was tied in a knot.
It had to be used. It was all that we had.
And, generally speakin' it wasn't so bad.

And the comb that hung down from a string underneath.
It was chuck full of gum though it lacked a few teeth,
And there on the bench was a rusty wash pan
Where we smeared yeller soap on our faces and hands.
The bosses them days didn't go for expense.
You could buy the whole outfit for ninty-five cents.

But boy let me tell you that old lookin' glass
Has reflected the faces of men with a past.
I wonder it didn't back up with surprise
If it read what was lurkin' just back of their eyes.
I will bet there's a lot of old hands can recall
The battered old mirror that hung on the wall.

Colts

I like to watch a bunch of mares
A grazin' on the plains.
And little colts with curious stares,
And fuzzy tails and manes.

Sometimes they touch their mother's nose.
Or scratch their little eyes.
And now and then they stand up close,
To keep away the flies.

Them little colts was might fleet
When it was time to travel,
The way them purty little feet
Could hit the sand and gravel.

And when a big hoss round up came
They'd run beside their mothers.
Them little colts they shore was game
And stayed right with the others.

And when the circle narrowed in,
'Twas then they made their show in'
When older hosses lost their wind,
The colts was up and goin'.

They shore was wild, them little brutes,
They wasn't raised fer pets,
But they was jest about as cute
as little critters gets.

The Coming Change

This here Injun is a watchin',
as he crouches on the plain,
And a hold in' to his pony
by a single rawhide rein.
It don't take him long to figger
what them covered wagons mean,
And to him a covered wagon,
is a mighty big machine.

When he sees a bunch of wagons,
or he finds a wagon track,
It is freighters or it's settlers,
and he's bein' crowded back.
But it wasn't just the Injun
that was crowded off the plain.
In a few more years the cowboy
got pushed off from his domain.

Grassy flats along the rivers
    where he bedded down his cows,
Was filled up with settlers' cabins,
    and turned under by their plows.
There was miles of open country
    he would never ride ag'in.
For the long barbed wire fences
fenced him out and fenced him in.

He was crowded into past'ers,
    and it wasn't many years,
Till the later settlers comin',
    crowded out the pioneers.
So they loaded up their wagons,
    and they started driftin' on;
Lookin' for a newer country,
    that lay somewhere out beyond.

So it is. Each generation has its
    chance and has its day.
Then the world goes on improvin'
    and is run a better way.
But we have the joy of know in'
    we have helped and done our share.
And when people tell what happened,
    we can say that we was there.

Cow Boy's Pants

You read and hear about the clothes
that cow boys used to wear.
The broad brimmed hats and high heeled boots,
you hear it every where.
The flannel shirt and handkercher,
but only just by chance
You ever hear or read a word about
a cow boy's pants.

Chorus.

They never mention pants by any circumstance,
But folks it's true I'm tellin' you that
cow boys did wear pants.

2.

Now over forty years ago
when in the camps I lit,
A cowboy wore just any kind of pants
that he could git.
A few of them was wearin' jeans
and some wore corduroys;
In fact most every kind of pants,
was found among the boys.

3.

But bye and bye there came a man
by name of Levi Strauss.
He started makin' overalls for men
that rode a hoss.
Old Levi knowed a cow boy
was soter thin and ga'nt
And so when Levi made them pants,
the laigs and seat was scant

4.

Most any hand you met with,
    from the wrangler to the boss,
Was wearin' them blue overalls
    put out by Levi Strauss.
When you saw a cow boy comin'
    you could gamble in advance,
That John B. Stetson made his hat,
    and Levi made his pants.

Cow Milkin'

Most cow boys aint handy at milkin' a cow.
In fact a whole lot of 'em never learned how.
What misses their vest, and their pants, and their pocket,
Goes up in their sleeve and runs back in the bucket

Besides that, most range cows ain't been dairy broke.
They know less about milkin' than any cow poke.
So, generally speakin', I reckon that's why
They don't git much milk and the cow soon goes dry.

This feller, he tied the calf up to the fence,
To git the milk started, and that showed good sense.
But right now "Old Bossy" has shore got him down,
With her foot in the bucket and messin' him 'round.

This boy must have wanted milk turrible bad,
Or he wouldn't have tried it. And won't he be mad?
He might beat the cow, but that won't be no use.
The best thing to do is to turn the calf loose.

The Cow-Boy's Dream

A cow-boy and his trusty pal
Were camped one night by an old corral;
They were looking for calves with lengthy ears,
And keeping a line on the boss's steers
The summer work was long since through
And only the winter branding to do.
When he went to rest there was frost on his bed,
But he pulled the tarp up over his head;
And into his blanket he burrowed deep—
He soon got warm and was fast asleep.
He dreamed he was through with his wayward past,
And had landed safe in Heaven at last.

A city was there, with its pearly gate,
And its golden streets were wide and straight.
The marble palaces gleamed and shone,
While the choir sang 'round the great white throne.
Outside there were trees and meadows green—
Such a beautiful range he had never seen.
Great rivers of purest waters flowed,
Though it never rained nor it never snowed.

He stood aside on the golden street,
There were heavy spurs on his booted feet,
His bat wing chaps were laced with whang,
But he listened and looked while the angels sang.
He noticed that he was the only one
With a broad brimmed hat and a big six gun.

So he said to a saint, "I'd shore admire
To be dressed like one of that angel choir.
Instead of these chaps and spurs and gun;
An' I reckon as how it could be done."
So they took him into a room aside
And fastened wings on his toughened hide.
They dressed him out in a flowing robe,

Like the lady who looks in the crystal globe.
They gave him a crown and a golden harp,
And the frost lay thick on the cow boy's tarp.

He twanged his harp and he sang a while,
Then he thought of something that made him smile.
For he was not one that sits and sings,
When they'd fitted him out with a pair of wings.
Said he "I reckon these wings would do
To show some mustangs a thing or two.
I'll jump a bunch and I'll flop and swoop,
I'll kick their tails and I'll yell and hoop;
I'll light a straddle of one of the things,
And I'll flop his flanks with my angel wings.
I'll ride him bare-back, but if I fail,
And he bucks me off, I'll simply sail."

He hunted wild horses in his dream,
But all he found was the chariot team.
That Old Elija drove in there,
And to pick on them would hardly be fair.
So he seated himself beneath a tree
And rested his crown upon his knee.
He watched the beautiful angels go—
Flying and fluttering to and fro.
At last one landed and started to walk—
She came up close and began to talk.
She had lovely hair of golden brown,
And was dressed in a flimsy silken gown.
She had dimpled cheeks and her eyes were blue,
And her fair white skin was beautiful too.

The cow-boy gazed at the angel's charms,
And attempted to clasp her within his arms.
"Stop! Stop!" she cried, "or I'll make complaints
To the great white throne and the ruling saints."
So the cow-boy halted, I must confess,
And failed to bestow that fond caress.
Said he: "Miss Angel, It's shore too bad,

This sort of a country makes me sad.
Where there ain't no night and it's always day,
And the beautiful ladies won't even play.
Where there's wonderful houses and golden streets,
But nobody sleeps and nobody eats.
Them beautiful rivers, it's sad to think,
There ain't no hosses nor cows to drink.
There is all this grass a-goin' to seed;
There ain't no critters to eat the feed.

A man can't gamble-there's so much gold
He could pick up more than his clothes would hold.
What's the use of the Judge and the great white throne,
Where troubles or fights was never known?
I'm sorry, miss, but I'll tell you true,
This ain't no place for a buckaroo."

Then she asked him about his former life,
She learned he had never possessed a wife.
But this angel lady, so sweet and nice,
Informed him that she had been married twice.
Her husbands had both been quiet men—
She thought if she had it to do again,
She'd have to decide between just two –
A sailor boy or a buckaroo.
She seated herself upon his knees,
And gave his neck such a hearty squeeze.
Just then he heard an excited call'—
Twas a gray old saint on the city wall.
He flopped his robes and he waved his arm
'Till the crowd all gathered in great alarm;
And then the cow-boy stood alone,
Before the judge and the great white throne.

"What's this?" the Judge of Creation cried;
"How come this fellow to get inside?
Age must be dimming St. Peter's eye
To let a spirit like that get by.
Just look at his face, with its desert brown,

And his bandy legs 'neath his angel gown.
He's a buckaroo,] know them well,
They don't allow them even in
Hell! He hasn't been here a half a day,
And he started an angel to go astray.
We can't permit him to stay a 'tall-
Just pitch him over the outside wall."
So the saints and the angels gave him a start
And he went toward the Earth like a falling dart.
But he never remembered the time he lit
For he wakened before the tumble quit.
The winter wind blew cold and sharp-
And the frost lay thick on the cow-boy's tarp.

His beautiful vision had come to grief,
So he baked his biscuit and fried some beef.
And he drank some coffee, black and strong;
But all that day as he rode along
He thought of the saint who had butted in,
And he said to himself (with a wicked grin);
"I wish'd had holt of that old saint chap,
I'd grab his whiskers and change his map.
I'd jump on his frame and stomp aroun'
'Till I tromped him out of his saintly gown."

And all his life, as he roamed and toiled,
He thought of his vision so sadly spoiled.
The meddlesome saint that caused it all
When he gave the alarm from the Jasper wall.
He didn't repent, nor he didn't pray,
But he always wished they'd let him stay.

The Cow Boy's If

If you can keep your head when all the cattle
Are breaking out and running through the brush.
If you can work like mad and not get rattled,
And ride a tired horse, but hold the rush.
If you can ride for long and weary hours
In summer storms that come a pouring down,
And then pay no attenion to these showers,
And wrestle calves upon the muddy ground.

If you can work in mountains rough and brushy
Or through the cactus on the desert sand.
Or wooded river bottoms soft and mushy,
And any where you go still make a hand;
If you can eat your breakfast in the dawning
And work as long as you can see the light,
Then crawl out of your blankets tired and yawning,
To take your turn at standing guard at night.

If you have no regard for how you're looking,
And seldom bathe and let your beard grow dense.
If you are good at butchering and cooking,
If you can shoe a horse or mend a fence;
If you can eat great gobs of beef and liver,
Or run a horse on any kind of ground;
If you can swim a herd across the river,
And not get any cows or horses drowned.

If you can race and head stampeded cattle
Through the darkness, pouring rain and pelting hail;
And then stay up all night to work and battle,
Or rope and tie a steer and seldom fail;
If you can learn to do team work with others,
Or winter brand upon the range alone,
Or trail through heat and dust that almost smothers
Or ride a bucking horse and not get thrown.

If you can catch a yearling calf and flank it;
Work with rope-burned hands but never flinch.
If you can kick the snow off of your blanket,
And whistle as you pull your frozen cinch.
If you can shoot and track just like a trapper,
If you can mend a riding gear that's wrecked,
And be good natured, but still be a scrapper
That any where he goes commands respect.

If you can fix a sweaty saddle blanket
So it won't hurt your horse to ride him hard.
If you can spend your pay and never bank it,
If you can stand to win or lose at cards.
If you can pack a horse with various matters
And throw your diamond hitch and pull the slack.
And fix it so it never slips or scatters,
Or so it will not hurt the horse's back.

If you can read a brand far in the distance,
Or work in country strange, and never stray.
If you can do all this without assistance,
And never quit the game but stay and stay.
If you can live on water that is dirty-
Too thick to swallow and too thin to chew.
You'll be an old man by the time you're thirty.
But then, my son, you'll be a cow-boy, too.

A Cowboy Funeral

There was once a cow boy funeral
that I many times recall.
A bad hoss killed a feller on a beef work
late one fall.
'Twas a bleak day in November
when the air was cold and raw.
The clouds looked gray and ugly,
and the wind blew down the draw.

There was no automobiles then,
and we was far from trains
In that rugged piece of country
where the canyons break the plains.
We had to make a buryin'
to finish the affair,
Well, the best time was the present,
and the closest place was there.

We hadn't any coffin,
and there was no bell to toll.
We went up on the hill side
and we dug a narrow hole.
We wrapped him up inside his bed
and laid him in the shale;
His saddle onderneath his head,
to ride the last long trail.

We had no book where we could look
and read of from its pages.
No one was there to say a prayer,
or sing the "Rock of Ages."
I recollect nobody spoke.
We didn't care to talk.
We filled the hole and took a smoke,
and raised a pile of rock.

And when the thing was over,
    it was soter like a dream,
How we helped the cook and wrangler
    while they harnessed up the team.
We got the herd mavin'
    and departed on our way.
And left that cow boy there to sleep,
    till resurrection day.

The Cowboys Christmas Dance

Winter is here and it aint so nice tendin'
　　the feeders and choppin' ice.
Nasty weather to stir about.
　　Cold in the morning's a gittin' out.
Puts a sting in your ears and nose;
　　gotta watch out or you'll freeze yore toes.
Blowin' your breath on a frosty bit.
　　Makes you feel like you want to quit.

You like one part of it any way,
　　that's when you git yore Christmas day.
Plenty of feed and a right good chance
　　to shake yore feet at a country dance.
Fiddles a playin' jest watch 'em go.
　　"Aleman left an' doce do!"
Don't keer none fer the cold and storms.
　　Dancin' around you soon git warm.

Folks all in from the hills and flats.
    Ears tied up onder their hats.
Tough on the hosses they drove and rode
    shivverin' there with their backs all bowed.
It's the only time that folks has to spare
    so the hosses had got to stand their share.
You turn 'em out when they git rode down
    but you got to keep workin' the year around.

Winter time but it aint so bad
    When it comes around yore sorter glad.
Even though it's nasty weather
    folks has a chance to git together.
And plenty of folks that was half way mad
    found out their neighbors was not as bad
Yes lots of trouble is checked in advance
    by a sociable crowd at a Christmas dance.

The Creak of the Leather

It's likely that you can remember
A corral at the foot of a hill
Some mornin' along in December
When the air was so cold and so still.
When the frost lay as light as a feather
And the stars had jest blinked out and gone.
Remember the creak of the leather
As you saddled your hoss in the dawn.

When the glow of the sunset had faded
And you reached the corral after night
On a hoss that was weary and jaded
And so hungry yore belt wasn't tight.
You felt about ready to weaken
You knowed you had been a long way
But the old saddle still kep a creakin'
Like it did at the start of the day.

Perhaps you can mind when yore saddle
Was standin' up high at the back
And you started a whale of a battle
When you got the old pony untracked.
How you and the hoss stuck together
Is a thing you caint hardly explain
And the rattle and creak of the leather
As it met with the jar and the strain.

You have been on a stand in the cedars
When the air was so quiet and dead
Not even some flies and mosquitoes
To buzz and make noise 'round yore head.
You watched for wild hosses or cattle
When the place was as silent as death
But you heard the soft creak of the saddle
Every time the hoss took a breath.

And when the round up was workin'
All day you had been ridin' hard
There wasn't a chance of you shirkin'
You was pulled for the second guard
A sad homesick feelin' come sneakin'
As you sung to the cows and the moon
And you heard the old saddle a creakin'
Along to the sound of the tune.

There was times when the sun was shore blazin'
On a perishin' hot summer day
Mirages would keep you a gazin'
And the dust devils danced far away
You cussed at the thirst and the weather
You rode at a slow joggin' trot
And you noticed somehow that the leather
Creaks different when once it gits hot

When yore old and yore eyes have grown hollow
And your hair has a tinge of the snow
But there's always the memories that follow
From the trails of the dim long ago.
There are things that will haunt you forever
You notice that strange as it seems
One sound, the soft creak of the leather,
Weaves into your memories and dreams.

The Dark Horse

Some troops were stationed at a fort,
Upon a reservation,
And just to have a little sport
And lively recreation,
They got two horses that could run
And built themselves a track.
The cash these sporting troopers won
Soon grew to quite a stack.
Old "Thunderinboots," the troopers
Had the fastest horse out west;
And "Oassin," a horse not bad,
They kept for second best.

Young "Howling-bull" came drifting in
And lounged about the fort-
A savage with a friendly grin,
Who liked to talk of sport.
For Howling-bull had just returned
From far-off eastern schools,
And if they taught him what he learned,
His teachers were no fools.

A bunch of Crows camped near the fort
Left 'twixt dark and dawn;
The soldiers were a race-horse short-
Old Thunderinboots was gone.
The troopers followed fast and hard-
They did not find the horse.
They offered quite a big reward
To get him back, of course.

Young Howling-bull, with stolid face,
Loafed in and out each shanty.
Before a week he matched a race
With his sorrel horse "Tegante."
They trained the troop-horse to his best,
Although it seemed absurd,
Because Tegante, with the rest,
Ran loose amongst the herd.

The redskins freely bet their furs
(They would have bet their hash);
They bet their ponies, ropes and spurs-
They hadn't any cash.
There'd get no cash, the soldiers feared,
Until that guileless soul,
The buck called "Howling-bull" appeared
And flashed a mighty roll.

The officers had much to say.
The settlers 'round him hovered;
They had to mortgage six months' pay
Before his bets were covered.

At last the day came for the race—
The soldiers dressed in blue;
And redskins swarmed about the place.
And all the settlers, too.
When bold young Howling-bull appeared.
He certainly looked quaint,
For man and horse were decked and smeared
With feathers, beads and paint.

Tegante wore four bright green socks —
'Twas plain enough to see.
They reached from fets and paster locks
Clear up to hock and knee.
A rawhide thong around his jaw —
No bridle on his head —
And as he turned the people saw
His face was painted red!

All through his mane and tail was tied
Long beaded buckskin strands;
And painted all about his hide
Were marks of human hands.
A half-grown boy came on the track–
As thin as any spider;
They tossed him on Tegante's back–
He was to be the rider.

The officers at once protest–
The soldiers gather 'round;
It gives Tegante all the best of weights,
By way of thirty pounds.
But Howling-bull does not debate–
He's out today for pelf;
He scorns to quibble on the weight,
And mounts the horse himself.
He throws his blanket on the ground
And pulls his breech-clout tighter.
That suits the people all around–
The jockey's much the lighter.

Down goes the flag – away they dart!
They leap with all their strength;
But see! The jockey has the start–
He's leading by a length!
Oassin's straining every nerve–
He's close against the rail.
And as they race around the curve,
They're running nose and tail.
Tegante cannot win the race,
The people say, of course.
The weight, the distance, and the pace,
Will kill the grass-fed horse.

But faster still Tegante goes,
Until they plainly see
He travels with his painted nose
Beside the jockey's knee.
They're going at a dreadful rate—
Oassin's running strong;
But Howling-bull throws half his weight
Against that rawhide thong.
Not half a length —not half a yard—
The trooper's horse can gain;
And still the redskin surges hard
Upon Tegante's rein.

Thus down the track the struggle goes—
A cheer the soldiers fetch,
As both the horses, nose to nose,
Swing out into the stretch.
Now Howling-bull begins to gain—
Ten seconds more they'll know;
The redskins slacks his single rein
And lets Tegante go.
In vain the jockey starts to flog—
He can't increase his speed;
As birch canoe would pass a log,
Tegante take the lead.

And fleeting like a painted ghost,
He leaves the thoroughbred,
And whizzes past the winning post
Some three good lengths ahead.

The crowd is gone — the fort is still—
The soldiers are all cross.
Six months must pass before
They will recover from their loss.
They're glum and cowed like green recruits
A shadow on each face,
For first they lost old Thunderinboots,
And then they lost the race.

Thus matters dragged on for awhile,
When Howling-bull appeared.
His heart seemed free from wicked guile,
And cheerfully he leered.
Old Thunderinboots the savage led,
And what do you suppose?
He paid a heavy price, he said,
To get him from the Crows.

Next morning, 'twas the groom, you see,
Excited their suspicion;
Hysterical he seemed to be,
And in a wild condition
"Come here, come here!" he loudly cried,
"And see what's to be seen.
Oh, Lord! that blessed Injun lied.
This water's all tuned green.
It happened when I washed his legs;
And when I washed his head.
Why, just as sure as eggs is eggs.
The water all turned red.

"He and Tegante both are sorrel
As like as twin and brother.
In fact, 't would make two strangers quarrel
To tell the one from 'tother.
He stole our horse off of the place—
He took him from the stall.
It was Thunderinboots that won that race,
And not his horse at all."

The curses called on Howling-bull
Were wicked, weird and strange;
But he was safe, with pockets full,
Out in the mountain range.
No pang of conscience or remorse
Disturbed his savage brest.
Because he'd raced their fastest horse
Against their second best.

The Disaster

There's troubles that keep a man fussin –
'There's sorrows that make his heart bleed.
But the thing that will set a man cuss in'
Is to see his old pack horse stampede.

He's a gentle old horse that you trusted–
You didn't expect it of him;
And that rotten old pack cinch got busted
When he tried to crowd under a limb.

He jumps and things start to scatter,
He snorts and then down goes his head;
You see right away what's the matter,
The pack rope is fast in your bed.

Your horse doesn't want to go near him,
The spurs doesn't alter his mind;
It'd make a'most any horse fear him,
With that object a draggin' behind.

You're swingin' your rope, and you're chargin',
But your horse won't go in for a throw;
He gives that pack horse a wide margin,
And that's just as close as he'll go.

He runs and he bucks without stoppin',
He's hangin' his tail on the moon,
While out of your "Kayacks" comes floppin'
Tomater cans, bacon and prunes.

Your fryin' pan sails like a rocket,
Your coffee pot lands in the rocks;
Some stuff you should have in your pockets,
You left in that pack in a box.

He certainly makes easy trailin'—
He leaves a broad track as he goes;
Fur out of your bed there comes sailin'
Tobacker and blankets and clothes.

Your tarp! Yes, of course, 'twas a new one,
But it's takin' on age mighty fast;
You can see everything that he's doin',
While the rocks and cedars flash past.

He falls, and gits wedged by a boulder,
He lays there all tremblin' and meek;
He's jimmed himself up in the shoulder—
Can't travel for over a week.

Your bed is all cactus and tatters,
Your stuff is strung out for a mile.
You recon there's plenty the matter—
You set down to figger a while.

There's troubles that keep a man fussin'
There's sorrow that make his heart bleed;
But the thing that will set a man cussin'
Is to see his old pack horse stampede.

Doing Her Best

This cow is in trouble, she's left on her own.
She has more than one cow can take care of alone.
She's protectin' her baby fer all she can do;
One wolf would be bad, but she's dealin' with two.

She can beller and call but there's no other cattle
To gather around her and help her do battle.
The calf's just a baby. There's no help in sight.
There is only one end for that kind of a fight.

The varmints feel sartin; they ain't in a hurry.
They will soon have that calf and they don't have to worry.
They could pull down the cow if they tried hard enough,
But the calf is a-plenty and not near so tough.

A wolf is a mighty mean varmint at heart.
He is cruel and wicked, and man! is he smart.
So I never could pity a wolf a whole lot
If he got in a trap. I was glad he got caught.

The Drag Driver

There's pictures and there's stories
    of the men that ride the lead.
He gives the herd direction
    and he regulates the speed.
There's pictures of the hands
    that ride along the flank and swing.
They hold 'em in and keep out strays
    and all that sort of thing.

I am speakin' of a rider
    on which nobody brags;
For man that must take grief and dust;
    the man that drives the drags.
To find a good drag driver
    ain't right easy so to speak.
He has got to handle cattle
    that are timid, slow and weak.

He dassen't be too easy
    and he dassen't be too rough.
He has got to savvy cattle
    and know when they've done enough.
If he crowds 'em too far forward
    why the others fight 'em back;
So he has to keep 'em movin'
    but allow 'em plenty slack.

He must have a lot of patience
    and a lot of judgment too.
It calls for mostly all he's got
    before the job is through.
Though he may use some salty words
    upon the ones that lags,
This man that follers up the herd,
    the man that drives the drags.

Drinkin' Water

When a feller once comes to a pond or a tank,
It is better to ride out a ways from the bank.
Fer the water is clearer out there as a rule,
And besides it is deep and a little more cool.

And out toward deep water, you notice somehow,
You miss a whole lot of that flavor of cow.
You can dip up a drink with the brim of yore hat,
And water makes purty good drinkin' at that.

You mebby spill some down the front of yore shirt,
But any old waddy knows that doesn't hurt.
There may be some bugs and a couple insecks
But it all goes the same down a cow puncher's neck.

I know there is plenty of folks would explain
Why such water had art to be filtered or strained.
Sech people as that never suffered from thirst,
Or they'd think of it later and drink it down first.

The Duel

Old Pan Handle Johnny was quick on the draw,
And a wonderful shot was old Billy McGraw.
Old Billy McGraw he expresed the belief
That Pan Handle Johnny was eatin his beef.

Well, Johnny got mad when he heard about that,
and he started to look fer where Billy was at.
And all kinds of wagers was goin' right soon,
When the boys laid their bets in the Lone Star saloon.

We knowed when they'd finished they'd only be one,
And some fellers bet that they wouldn't be none.
The only thing gave 'em reason to bet,
Was the lay of the land when the two fellers met.

If they fought at close quarters or after 'twas night,
Well, Pan Handle Johnny would finish the fight.
But take it in daylight at thirty five paces
Old Billy could shoot the spots out of the aces.

They was ten steps apart when them two fellers met.
The sun had gone down but it wasn't dark yet.
Johnny fired four shots before Billy could draw.
Three of 'em went wild and one shot hit McGraw.

Old Billy shot once and he knocked Johnny dead
Then he deemized plum sudden the bystanders said.
And the fellers all won that had bet on a draw
Between Pan Handle Johnny and Billy McGraw.

Feedin' Time

You are warm in the cabin, and doin' yore cookin'
But you know that yore hosses are there, without lookin'.
It's long about time they come into be fed
And to be put away fer the night in the shed.

Both hosses and mules seem to have their own way
Of tellin' exactly the time of the day.
And I've noticed besides they don't ofen git lost,
Like some human bein's you've happened acrost.

Yore feet is so warm that you don't like to go
And git yore boots wet wadin' 'round in the snow.
But it's feed makes 'em stout, and it's feed brings 'em back:
So you pull on yore boots, and you start makin' tracks.

You pull down yore hat and you turn up yore collar.
You start fer the shed and the hosses both faller.
They are glad to see you, and I've generally found,
A man don't git so lonesome with hosses around

Figger It Out

There's a big Christmas package hung up on the fence.
This Cow Pony thinks that it doesn't make sense.
He shows mighty plain jest the way that he feels,
'Bout that big paper box and its bright Christmas seals.

Old cow boy, it's got you to figgerin' too.
Yore head. You don't know what to do.
That box is too big to tie on by the string.
It might break, or git shook till you ruint the thing.

If yore hoss breaks in two he's a hard one to ride.
You caint do it and carry that package beside.
If he starts in to buck, it's a mighty good chance
You'll be facin' the sky with the seat of yore pants.

Besides you have got quite a long ways to go.
You don't want to do it on foot in the snow.
Yes, yore hoss is plum hostile about the affair.
He don't know about Christmas; what's more he don't care.

The Fight In The Dark

You loosen the cinches to let your hoss blow
While you look for the ranch in the valley below.
You can make it out plain at the foot of the hill,
Down there in the starlight all quiet and still.
Ain't nobody stirrin'. It seems sort of strange.
They are reckoned some spread on this neck of the range.

It's early and yet they ain't burnin' no light.
You follered the trail like they told you all right.
It must be the place. There's a flash in the dark!
And up from below comes a six shooter's bark!
Two others break out on the left and the right,
And a wicked tongued rifle cuts into the fight.

There's a hoarse chokin' yell. Yes, some feller got hit.
Things ain't no ways peaceful down there, not a bit.
The echoes wake up and the mountains shore ring.
There's another old rifle beginnin' to sing.
Down close to the cook shack comes ugly and short,
The dull heavy sound of a shot gun's report.

From the door of the bunk house you see the long streaks
Where the flame stabs the air as a Winchester speaks.
There is a couple more six guns a talkin' right mean,
And sharp like a whip cracks a saddle carbeen.
There is one thing plum sartin, the ranch is attacked.
They tried to sneak up, and got ketched in the act.

Jest what was the trouble and how did it start?
Never mind, yore a stranger around in these parts.
And you want to remember, whoever wins out
Won't care fer no strangers a hangin' about.
The best thing fer you is to start rollin' yore tail,
And be makin' some tracks down along the back trail.

You will the yarn told by the camp fire some night,
Of the raid on the ranch, and the free for all fight.
Yore a whole lot more likely to live to be old
If you l'arn about fightin' from hearin' it told.
And nosin' around when there's feuds on the range
Is mighty onhealthy for folks that is strange.

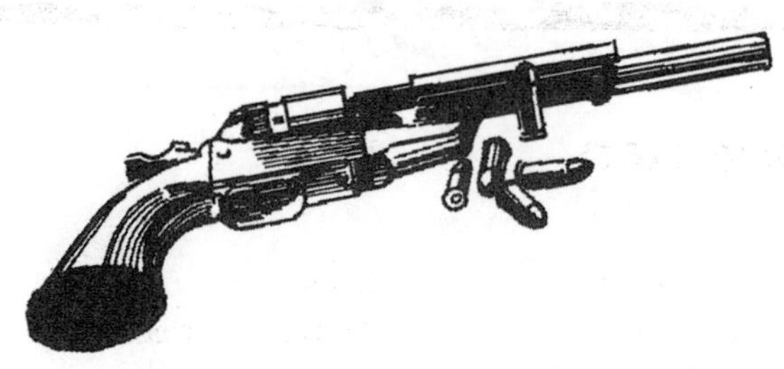

Forgotten

Yes, he used to be a cow hoss
that was young and strong and fleet
Now he stands alone, forgotten,
in the winter snow and sleet.
Fer his eyes is dim and holler
and his head is turnin' gray,
He has got too old to foller
"Jest a hoss that's had his day."

They've forgotten how once he packed 'em
at a easy swingin' lope.
How he braced his sturdy shoulders
when he set back on a rope.
Didn't bar no weight nor distance;
answered every move and word,
Though his sides were white with lather
while he held the millin' herd.

Now he's stiff and old and stumbles,
    and he's lost the strength and speed
That once took him through the darkness,
    'round the point of a stampede
And his legs is scarred and battered;
    both the muscle and the bone.
He is jest a wore out cow hoss
    so they've turned him out alone.

They have turned him out to winter
    best he can amongst the snow.
There without a friend and lonesome,
    Do you think he doesn't know?
Through the hours of storm and darkness
    he has time to think a lot.
That hoss may have been forgotten,
    but you bet he aint forgot.

He stands still. He aint none worried,
    fer he knows he's played the game
He's got nothin' to back up from.
    He's been square and aint ashamed.
Fer no matter where they put him
    he was game to do his share
Well, I think more of the pony
    than the folks that left him there.

The Gentle Hoss

Of all the things you come across,
the best one is a gentle hoss.
A man don't have to git a rope
and ketch him on the flyin' lope,
And mebby have to ear him down,
and git all shook and jerked around.
And mebbyso git kicked or throwed
before he gits the critter rode.

A gentle hoss is shore a pal.
You walk into the hoss corral,
You take yore bridle in yore hand
and he's so gentle that he'll stand.
He doesn't fight the bit aytall,
and when you put on the head stall,
He doesn't seem to have no fears.
He knows you won't rough up his ears.

He doesn't fret and fight and fuss,
like some ill tempered onery cuss.
He's with you all the long day through
to help with what you have to do.
And any time you rope and tie,
he'll hold the slack and shore stand by.
In case your workin' on the ground,
jest drop the reins, he'll stick around.

Jest think the time and work he saves;
this gentle pony that behaves.
A cow boy mighty soon will find
he's worth three of the other kind.
He wants to work and do his share
and never quits you any where.
Of all the things you come across,
the best one is a gentle hoss.

Ghost Canyon Trail

There are strange tales told of spirits bold,
And the trail to Santa Fe,
There is many a tale of the Chisholm trail,
And the trail to Laramire.
But this is the tale of an obscure trail.
That few men travelled on;
Where a spirit was known to ride alone,
'Twixt the midnight hour and dawn.

It would wind and creep through canyons deep
And over the mesa wide.
The men who knew this trail were few,
Where the phantom used to ride.
At times was heard a careless word
Some drinking man let fall,
But 'twas held a joke by the rangeland folk,
That no one believed atall.

I learned the truth from a hardy youth.
He was one of those reckless men
Who could ride in the lead of a night stampede,
Or the dust of the broncho pen.
On a winter night when the stars were bright
And the dying moon was low,
He was holding his course on a jaded horse
And the pace that he made was slow.

The cow horse flinched and cringed, till the cinch
Was almost against the ground.
His quivering ears showed deathly fear
And the cow boy looked around.
He felt the thrill of a clammy chill,
As it travelled along his spine,
For he saw at his side a phantom ride,
With never a word or sign.

He kept his place, for he set his pace
To the cow boy's jogging speed,
There came no sound on the frozen ground
From the tread of his phantom steed.
He showed a flash of a long mustache
And a tilted campaign hat,
There straight and strong with stirrups long
The phantom trooper sat.

They were all alone. And the pale moon shone
Through the ghost at the cow boy's side.
His courage fled as he rode with the dead
Alone on the mesa wide.
No sign of flight, no show of fight
The buckaroo displayed,
For slugs of lead won't hurt the dead,
Through the mist of a vapor shade.

With the mesa past they came at last
To a canyon wide and dark,
Where some stone huts stood in the cottonwoods
That had long been an old land mark.
Each ruined shack had a chimney black,
And a roofless crumbling wall.
A living spring, was the only thing
That was useful to men atall.

The chilling breezes through the leafless trees,
Gave a dreary dismal moan.
The trooper stayed in the ghastly shade
And the cow boy rode alone.
Strange tales are heard of what occurred
At that place in years gone by,
Ere that restless soul of the night patrol
Rode under the starlit sky.

What the trooper knows, or where he goes,
Nobody has ever found.
But the tale is told of the lone patrol
By the older settlers 'round.
There's a cow boy trim with a face that's grim,
Will never forget that ride
On a winter night in the pale moon light,
By the phantom trooper's side.

The Ghosts at the Diamond Bar

'Twas a winter night at the Diamond Bar,
The wind was blowin' cold.
The Dipper swung 'round the dim North Star
And the night was growin' old.
But I had some wood that was dry and good,
So I let the cold wind whine.
I was safe and snug with a gallon jug
Of Death Valley Slim's moonshine.

Across the stove from where I sat
Stood a figger straight and tall.
He had no coat, he had no hat,
He must have come through the wall
He pointed away toward a rocky shelf
That was up on the side of a hill.
He was one of the bunch the Injuns skelped
When they raided the old ore mill.

I nodded and passed the gallon jug.
He needed a drink or two.
But he only shrugged and shook his head;
That was sumpthin' he could not do.
I set the jug down on the floor;
Then my eyes popped open wide.
There had been jest one; now a couple more
Was a stand in' there by his side.

They would each one point with a ghostly hand
Where my old harmonica lay.
By signs they made me understand
They wanted that I should play.
So I played 'em "The Grave On The Lone Prairie,"
And "The Dyin' Ranger" too.
And twenty odd ghosts surrounded me
Before I was half way through.

I played 'em the old "Rye Whisky" tune
And they waltzed it 'round and 'round.
But I felt no weight on the floor of the room
And their feet made never a sound.
Then "Rosie O'Grady" and "Over The Waves,"
They waltzed with keen delight.
Them wandering spirits out of their graves
Was havin' a time that night.

They motioned that I should drink once more.
That was easy to understand.
With noiseless feet, they stomped the floor
And patted their phantom hands.
When I seen 'em smile I changed my style.
I played old "Larry McGee."
They wanted something with a lilt and swing,
And they stepped it light and free.

But jest as the thing was gain' grand,
There was sumpthin' spoiled the show.
There wasn't a drop in the coal oil can
And the lamp was burnin' low.
I stopped and drunk me a hefty slug
And a thought come to mind.
I filled the lamp from the moonshine jug
And she blazed like a neon sign.

There was battered hats on the buckaroos.
Old miners with unshaved jaws.
Three Wallapi bucks were in there too,
And a couple Mohave squaws.
The next was the old time "Chicken Reel,
And you'd orta seen 'em go.
They would jig on the corners before they'd wheel
And give it the heel and toe.

I knew they wouldn't be there fer long.
It would soon be breakin' day.
And I wanted to sing 'em a good old song
Before they went on their way.
So I sung like I had never sung before,
Till the last of the crowd was gone.
And when I opened the ranch house door,
The day was beginning to dawn.

Yes, the desert trails have their own weird tales
That few of us mortals know.
And I'll never forget that crowd I met
On that night so long ago.
Some time I will meet them again, maybe,
Though I don't know where they are.
But why did they come to visit me,
That night at the Diamond Bar?

Graves By The Side Of The Trail

When the trail herds came through
And the wagon trains too
And the stage coach that carried the mail
They were brave hardy souls
But the West took it's toll
For it's graves by the side of the trail.

CHORUS

On the tough mountain side,
On the lone prairie wide,
'Neath the trees in some broad grassy swale,
In the land of the West
They have gone to their rest
In their graves by the side of the trail.

There were redskins to fight
There were fierce outlaws white
There were sick ones whose strength seemed to fail
Others perished alone
And were buried unknown
In their graves by the side of the trail.

There's a great judgment day
At the last so they say
When the Earth and the Heavens unveil,
God will call them and then
They will rise once again
From their graves by the side of the trail.

The Gray Wolf

The stockman lay in his blanket bed
We were sleeping, he and I.
We each one wakened-he raised his head
At the sound of a gray wolfs cry.

He knew the sound of that dismal yell—
He knew that it boded ill;
For that long drawn wail like a howl from Hell,
Was the cry of a wolf at his kill.

Next day we found near a ledge of stone,
Where a yearling gamely fought.
The wolf had tom the flesh from the bone,
To feast while the meat was hot.

He had left his victim tom and scarred,
Though it quivered still with life;
Then the stockman's eye grew bright and hard
Till it shone like the blade of a knife.

He carefully laid a line of traps—
He tracked with a ready gun.
Said he: "We will get him some day, perhaps."
But the gray wolf always won.

He seemed to wander and rove at will
Through that rugged, arid land;
And whenever he chose he made his kill,
Regardless of mark or brand.

His great wide track was everywhere,
And I saw his victims bleed
Till I cursed the heart, the hide and the hair
And the spawn of the gray wolf's breed.

So this warfare of cunning-weird and strange—
Went on from day to day;
And at night, far up in the mountain range,
Rang the powerful, deep-toned bay.

One summer morning, just after: dawn
I found a sign quite plain;
For one of the stockman's traps was gone,
With its drag and the heavy chain.

We saw the tracks of his first mad rush,
Then the mark of claw and fang,
Where he tore the earth and broke the brush,
Wherever the clog would hang.

He was close by the bank of a dried-up stream—
He did not whine or flinch.
His eyes shone hard with an evil gleam,
And he did not retreat an inch.

For a moment we gazed when our prey we found,
But he silently faced we two.
With never a sound he stood his ground,
And died like a rustler true.

The stockman's hand gave an easy sweep—
He balanced his heavy gun.
The pistol spoke with a bark and a leap,
And the great gray wolf was done.

He had lived in that beautiful coat of hair,
Unhampered in race or fight;
Immune to the desert's heat and glare,
Or the storms on the coldest night.

Useless, at last, were those padded feet,
With tendons that never tire;
On the roughest ledge they were swift and fleet —
They could race over bog and mire.

And the yellow eyes with their evil gleam,
That could see by night and day;
And the deep strong chest that had hurled each scream,
Or driven his deep-toned bay.

And the cruel head so full – so proud –
That could plan with such fiendish skill;
I wondered a creature thus endowed,
Should only be meant for ill.

We stripped the hide from his body lean–
I marveled at what I saw;
The wonderful muscles, long and clean,
And the powerful neck and jaw.

The great jaw teeth that could crush the bone,
Or hang at their owner's will;
They were sharp as the edge of a jagged stone,
And the fangs that could slash and kill.

The shoulder wide and the mighty limb,
That could last through the longest race;
And yet, with all he was lithe and trim
A model of strength and grace.

He had used his gifts as their giver meant –
He was not endowed for good.
He's true to the last, and when he went –
He died as a gray wolf should.

The Hacamore Colt

When a hacamore colt starts to learnin'
The ways and the methods of men;
He gits skeert, and sometimes without warnin'
He starts off to buckin' again.

He listens and looks when you're talkin',
Although he don't know what you say.
His is puzzled a heap by your walkin';
He don't know that two legged way.

When you pull out a sack of the makin's,
He doesn't like that perty well.
He mebbyso snorts and starts shakin'
Because he don't savvy that smell.

And when a man acts like he itches,
When he rakes down his leg with a scratch,
And the fire flies out of his britches,
The colt doesn't know it's a match.

He fidgets, he pulls and he fusses,
He drives a man into a rage.
He is one of them ignorent cusses,
But what did you know at his age?

And so I have soter concluded,
There ain't any call to git sore,
He knows a heap more than what you did,
When you was along about four.

Her Neighbor's Kids

Most cows will give their calves good care.
They make the best of mothers
She knows her own calf anywhere
Among a hundred others.

But if a strange calf muzzles in
He finds out mighty quick.
She moves him out from there ag'in,
And does it with a kick.

It ain't because she hates that calf
She starts to gittin' rough.
But if she cuts her milk in half,
Her own won't have enough

There ain't a lot he understands
When he's too young fer weanin',
But any time a hard kick lands
You bet he gits the meanin'.

Cows don't git out and lead parades
Nor speak fer missionaries.
She hasn't got no ladies' aides,
Nor no auxiliaries.

She has a calf that's all her own.
She's tryin' to git by.
She figgers to be let alone
Or know the reason why.

High An' Wicked

When they cut you out a bucker
why the boys all gathers 'round
Fer to see the hull performance
when you let the hammer down,
They will help you while you saddle
and they ear him down you bet,
Till they git you up a straddle
and you tell 'em that yore set.

Then they jump away and holler
and they hit him with their hat,
And he bucks plum high and wicked
weavin' crooked like a bat.
When he hits the ground he shakes you,
then he lurches though the air –
You caint see that broncho no place
but you shore can feel he's there.

Now you aim to show that critter
they's a cow boy on his back
So you rake him down the shoulders
and you pitch the cuss the slack.
Then you show the other fellers
how you fan 'em with yore lid,
And the old hoss bucks and bellers
while you hollar like a kid.

Now yore gittin' kinda dizzy
and yore feelin' sorter shook;
You was sartin you could ride him
but you might have been mistook.
But his jumps begin to weaken
and at last his head appears;
It's a welcome sight old cowboy,
is a buckin' hosse's ears.

Honest John's Five Aces

Things was goin' soter quiet
    on a lazy afternoon,
And us boys was playin' poker
    down to Andy Blunt's saloon.
Even the air around us
    had a soter peaceful feelin'
And old "Honest John" the gambler
    was the feller that was dealin'.

A stranger came a bustin' in,
    a mask was on his face.
He hollered at us "Stick 'em up"!
    He aimed to rob the place.
He showed mighty little judgment
    when he tied into that crowd
Fer the fellers down at Andy's
    wasn't very easy cowed.

No, There wasn't any talkin'
    cept the language of the "Colts"
And the atmosphere was rockin'
    to the sharp and heavy jolts.
And we noticed some time later
    that place was shore a wreck
Them there bullets broke the mirrirs
    and they busted bottle necks.

Andy tried to grab his shot gun
    but he couldn't reach that far
'Cause he'd left his sawed off shot gun
    at the tother end the bar.
There was several of our number
    when the smoke had cleared away
Layin' in eternal slumber
    waitin' fer the judgment day.

Well the hold up man was finished.
One man laid there in his gore
But, a hand that showed five aces
laid face upward on the floor.
Well, it didn't take no guess in'
we could easy onderstand
But we heard some harsh expressions
'bout the man that held the hand.

It aint right to knock a feller
that has crossed the great devide.
But you know that crooked gamblin'
shore gits onderneath the hide
There is things that plum disgraces
even them that's dead and gone
Yes, the hand that held five aces
had belonged to Honest John.

Hoof Beats

In the song of the West, each tune and word,
Should be set to the tread of the pony herd.
It dates from the time the dust clouds rose
From the travelling herd of buffaloes,
And the mounted red skinned hunter came
To pursue and slaughter this mighty game.
With the rush of the herd as the hunters come,
Sound the horses' feet, with their drum drum drum.

Then out of the mountains and o'er the plain,
The trapper came with his laden train,
To the trading post with the spoils he'd brought.
He came at a walk and a shuffling trot.
In single file they followed the track,
And each horse carried his heavy pack.
The trappers and traders used to come;
Hear the horses' feet with their drum drum drum.

The frontier army-only groups
Of reckless men in cavalry troops.
Walk, trot, and gallop. That was their gait.
Fearless riders sitting straight.
Those tiny forts and garrisons small,
But the blue clad riders held them all.
A cheer for the troopers! Here they come,
The horses' feet with their drum drum drum.

The emigrant train, where the oxen toil,
And the wagon wheels cut into the soil.
They form a circle-They hear the shouts
Of the flanking herders and mounted scouts.
They form a circle and make a stand,
To fight for their lives with the raiding band.
To the sound of the war whoop, Here they come!
The ponies' feet with their drum drum drum.

And then, the Texans sallied forth,
With their long homed herds toward the fertile North.
In the night, the storm, and the mad stampede,
These daring riders would "Bend the lead."
The dare devil cow boys, here they come!
The horses' feet with their drum drum drum.

The mining camp, with its toil and thrills.
The stage coach comes through the rugged hills.
The brake shoes rasp as they rock and ride
At a reckless pace down the mountain side.
The freighter comes with his long line team.
The heel chains clank and the brake blocks scream.
The wagons and coaches, here they come,
And the horses' feet with their drum drum drum.

The jaded steeds of an outlaw gang.
The vigilanties that shoot and hang.
The desperadoes brought to bay,
Where the rifles and six guns said their say.
The men who fought till their parting breath,
As their hard eyes glared in the jaws of Death.
The powder cracks, and the bullets hum,
And the horses' feet with their drum drum drum.

When the cattle and sheep men settled a score
Without the law, in a fierce range war.
They battled it out with heart and soul,
At a cabin, a butte or a water hole.
Some stock man, outnumbered and crowded hard,
Was waiting to play his final card,
But there's help at last, for here they come!
The horses' feet with their drum drum drum.

A couple of reckless unkempt men,
In the welter and dust of the broncho pen.
A bucking horse as he leaps and groans,
Till he fairly wrenches the rider's bones.
The saddle that creaks on its cinches tight
These wild young horses knew how to fight.
Sometimes they can shake their rider numb
Ere their quick feet cease with their drum drum drum.

And now, through the land of winding trails,
Run concrete highways, and long steel rails.
But the western horse, that played his part,
With wiry muscles, and valiant heart,
Will hold his place in the stirring past,
So long as the pages of history last:
Through the engine's roar and the motor's hum,
Drown the sound of his feet, with their drum drum.

Hook 'Em Cow

You read of fierce bulls in the stories and books,
But you don't hear a heap 'bout an old cow that hooks
A bull charges blind, but an old cow is wise.
She keeps her head shakin' and opens her eyes.
If you git to a post I have generally found
She runs right up to it and reaches around.

And yore bid din' fer trouble as shore as yore born
If you git yore old belly mixed up with her horn.
You have seen a cow scatter a whole brandin' crew
When they drug a calf in and the cow follered too.
Think a cow boy caint run? Well you aint seen one sail
When a cow blows her nose on some waddy's shirt tail.

Sometimes when you pull a cow out of a bog
She will charge with a rush like some salty brush hog.
If an old cow gits down cause she's weak and she's pore,
If you help git her up she will fight you jest shore.
If you judge by her actions toward hosses and men,
She's by nature a heap like an old settin' hen.

I'll bet you was glad that you wasn't too late
When you lit with yore belly across some old gate,
And an old cow hit right underneath with a crash.
Jest a little more and she'd settled yore hash.
You fell on across, and was mad when you heered
How the rest of them ranch hands hollered and cheered.

Yes cows is odd critters; it shore is plum strange.
The pet cows is gentle, but them on the range
Is a sp'ilin' fer fight if they once git a skeer,
Or you make a calf bawl when the old cow can hear.
They're onreasonable cusses I'll tell you right now,
Fer you caint explain much to a fightin' old cow.

The Hoss Round Up

The circle is throwed and yore closin' in,
The day is quiet and hazy.
You know the fun -is about to begin,
They're a takin' 'em off of the mesa.
There's plenty of hosses comin' in sight
Yore old hoss seems to know.
He feels you pullin' the cinch up tight
And he's slingin' his head to go.

You must turn 'em now or they'll double back.
The time has come to ride.
You raise in yore stirrups and ease him some slack
As you settle him into his stride.
You have saved yore hoss to the very last
But now it has come to a show
The rocks, the brush and the trees flash past
And the ground is a blur below.

Some of the mares have colts at their heels,
Plum fast no use denyin'
You can hear the neighs, the snickers and squeals,
The manes and the tails are flyin' .
They charge right on through a gopher town
Their hoofs beat a steady rumble.
A cloud of dust as a hoss goes down
And a couple of others stumble.

You bust a snag when it rakes yore knee
But it loosens you up in the saddle.
There's part of yore shirt on a cedar tree
And yore warmin' up to the battle.
And now they are over the mesa's edge
Through the brush you see them flashin' .
The loosened rocks go over the ledge
You can hear them a rollin' and crashin'.

The boys below is closin' in.
They ain't fell down on the job.
They gathered the "Maichies" out of the rims
An they're throwin' them into the mob.
Yore hoss cold jaws when he hears them yell.
No chance to hold him in.
He slips in the rocks, he almost fell
But he's up and he's runnin' agin.

You are down to the wash and into the sand
And up on the other side.
The cat claw tears at yore face and hands,
Like a bat out of Hell you ride.
You know they are takin' you too far South
But yore still in the race and streakin'
You can taste the sweat and dust in yore mouth
And yore hoss is beginnin' to weaken.

You can feel that yore mount is about all in,
But the bunch is down to a lope.
If you kick or spur you will get his wind
So you flog with a double of rope.
'Twas the last he had but he won with that
You kept the bunch together,
And you all go lumberin' out on the flat
Where the old hands is holdin' the "Prather".

Their mounts are fresh and they onderstand,
They are racin' like mad to meet 'em
They know every trick of a broncho band
And savvy the way to beat 'em.
The prather hosses are gentle too,
They are fresh and a whole lot faster.
They circle 'em in and they drift 'em through
And the herd goes into the paster.

At last the boys that have made the run
Ride slowly up together;
Their tremblin' mounts are about all done,
They are pantin' and covered with lather.
The boys are stiff when they clamber down,
And they walk with a rollin' stride.
They twist up smokes as they stumble around
Knees bent and feet spread wide.

There are two men short but at last they show.
Their wore out hosses laggin'.
They are takin' it easy and travelin' slow
With their cinches loose and saggin'.
The boss shoves his old hat back on his head,
His face wears a friendly grin.
"I'm glad we have got that bunch" he said
"They're a little bit hard to bring in."

How a Cow Puncher Rode

I have often been asked by the people I knowed,
To tell 'em the way that a cow puncher rode.
Now them cow hands they didn't all ride jest the same.
They rode a'most every old style you could name.

Of course, most of the hands that was workin' around,
Would ride with long stirrups, and straight up and down.
Some rode with 'em medium, some rode with 'em short.
In fact there was stirrups, and len'ths of all sorts.

I know of one feller that quarreled with his brother,
Because he rode with one stirrup longer than t'other.
Some stuck their laigs foreward and held their heels low.
Some held their laigs back and turned down their toe.

Some held their feet still, but some figity cuss
Would keep kick in' his feet and makin' a fuss.
There was some that set straight,
but there's others that humped
Till they set on their hoss as a sort of a lump.

There was some of them riders kep' close to their seat.
While others was half of the time on their feet.
Some bogged on the cantel and rode away back,
While others would jig like they rode on a tack.

There was some kep' their elbows down close to their side.
And others ag'in that would let 'em spread wide.
While some of 'em flopped up their elbows so high,
You would think mebbyso they was tryin' to fly.

There was them that would ride with their hand on the horn.
Some looked plum contented and some looked forlorn.
There was them, fer some reason I couldn't explain,
Whirled a piece of their rope or the end of a rein.

There was some of them fellers set off to one side.
In fact I can't tell how a cow boy did ride.
When I figger it out, their is only one guess.
They rode like they thought they could do it the best.

(Borein)

How They Made the Royal Gorge

Did you ever hear how "Brindle"
that old long horn Texas steer
Drifted into Colorado
long before the gorge was here
He was old and he was foxy
he was fast and he was tough
And he never struck a mountain
where the going was too rough.

The cow boys used to chase him
he was never ketched and tied
He'd go down the river
swim across and take the other side
He never left the river bottom
because that critter knowed
He could outrun all the ponies
that them cow boys ever rode.

He'd go up and down a mountain
and he didn't keer how steep
He'd go over rocks and boulders
faster than a mountain sheep
If you jumped him in the open
he could give you spades and cards
He could spot a rabbit fifty feet
and race him fifty yards.

Then Dutch George come to the country
with a string of sixty head
Cream of all the saddle hosses
so the early settlers said.
He had mules to do his packin'
that he didn't never ride
He kep a wrangle pony
and a Sunday hoss beside.

Now Dutch George he jumped Old Brindle
 and he gave him quite a run
But he left Dutch George behind him
 long before the day was done
Then Old George he lit in cussin'
 fer it made him awful mad
And he swore he'd ketch old Brindle
 or kill every hoss he had.

So George fenced him up a paster
 where the grass was tall and thick
Said he'd camp right in that country
 till at last he'd done the trick
When he took to chasin' Brindle
 that old critter was amazed
Cause George had so many hosses
 he could rest 'em sixty days.

Well George chased him all the summer
 all the winter and the spring
And it kept him busy rid in'
 all the horses in his string
Every morning after breakfast
 George would bight him off a chaw
Then he'd take and chase Old Brindle
 up and down the Arkansaw.

They'd knock dirt into the river
 which the current washed away
And the trail kept gittin older,
 it got broader day by day
After several years of runnin'
 why their trail got awful deep
In among the cliffs and boulders
 and the sides got high and steep.

George's hosses started dyin',
    George was gittin' old and gray,
And his wife she died and left him,
    still that old steer kept away
But Old George he never weakened
    for he got hisself a squaw
And he kep on a chasin' Brindle
    up and down the Arkansaw.

So fer years they kep a runnin'
    and before the race was done
They tramped out sech a canyon
    that they never saw the sun
George he run plum out of hosses
    and the day the last one dropped
He was left afoot and walkin'
    but you bet he never stopped.

Up and down that rocky canyon
    they kep on another year
Several times along toward evenin'
    George he almost ketched the steer
Both his boots was worn to ribbons
    and his feet was sore and raw
But he stayed right after Brindle
    up and down the Arkansaw.

Then one evenin' jest at sunset
    they found George a layin' dead
And Old Brindle laid a dyin'
    twenty seven feet ahead.
Yes Old Brindle won the contest
    but that stubborn Dutchman George
Chased him up and down the river
    till they'd dug the Royal Gorge.

The Joshua Shade

Did you ever start out fer to make a long ride
When the sun was so hot it was fryin' yore hide?
And along about noon you could feel yore blood bile
And yore hoss was so hot you must rest him a while.

Where about all the shade that a feller could see
Was the top and the trunk of a joshua tree.
When you got on the ground you could shore feel the heat.
It went plum through yore boots and was hurtin' yore feet.

The hoss got the shade of the top, and you laid
Between him and the tree in a slim strip of shade.
He stood plenty quiet, a shuttin' his eyes,
Too hot and too tired to fight off the flies.

All around you as far as a feller could look
The air was so hot that it shivered and shook.
The lizzards denned up and the crows wouldn't fly,
And only a buzzard sailed 'round in the sky.

Well they say that the sun is what makes the world go.
It keeps people healthy, makes everything grow,
Now all of these wonderful things may be true,
But it gits plenty hot fer to kill a man too.

Judgement Day

Once I dremt while I was sleepin'
That the earth had passed away,
And the boss of all creation
Made a work on Judgment Day,
They was folks of every color
They was folks of every breed
And they cut' em into bunches
'Cordin' to their race and creed.

Top hand angels done the cuttin'
They knowed how to handle things,
Some would change and help the others
While they'd smoke and rest their wings.
And I seed a bunch of fellers
They was holdin' on the side.
Grazin' soter loose and easy
And the angels workin' wide.

He had judged and classed the others
By a book of rules he used,
Then he called out to the angels
"Now bring on the buckaroos!"
Angels bunched and shoved 'em foreward,
Some surprised but not dismayed.
Amblin' up to face the judgment
Came that grizzled wild brigade.

Each one pulled his hat on tighter
That they done from habit's force,
It's a trick of most rough riders
When they mount a buckin' horse.
Some was young and some was older,
Some walked with a limpin' stride.
Some still had the high healed boots on
They was wearin' when they died.

They all stood in line to answer
Fer the way they'd spent their days.
And they faced the boss of Heaven
With a cool and level gaze.
And the boss of all creation
Give them boys a kerful look,
And sez to a top hand angel,
"Bring me out that range law book."

Well, I turned and asked an angel
Why the judgment book was changed,
And they judged that bunch of cow boys
By the laws that ruled the range.
And he answered very solemn
That the reason was because
You could never judge a cow boy
By another feller's laws.

The Line Camp

You rode into the line camp 'bout the
time the sun went down;
Got the load from off yore pack hoss,
throwed yore saddle on the ground.
You was glad the man before you
had a heart and chopped some wood,
But when you went inside the shack
things wasn't quite so good.

You found dead flies and cobwebs
and lots of things like that.
One stove laig broke, some wore out clothes,
and plenty sign of rats.
You got a rock and propped the stove
and soter cleaned the junk.
Then drug yore tarp and blankets in
and throwed them on the bunk.

Next thing you brought your grub inside
and built a fire on.
There wasn't any lantern
and the candles all was gone.
Well, you tore up some flannin rags
and made a right good wick,
And scouted out a lard pail lid –
you waddies know the trick.

You melted taller or some lard,
it didn't matter which;
And you was all primed up to go,
you had a "Kitchen Bitch."
The coffee cooked, the meat got fried,
and you was cheerful hearted.

Because you had been there before
    and soter liked the shack.
The same old nails to hang yore clothes,
    the rafters smoky black.
And when you got yore supper et
    you lit yore pipe agin,
Then propped yore feet up by the
    stove and let the heat soak in.

Before you slept you went to see
    your night hoss in the trap.
You crawled into yore blankets
    and you didn't give a rap.
The night wind blowed real soft and slow
    and you was all alone;
It was nothin' but a line camp
    but to you 'twas home sweet home.

The Long Eared Bull

The long-eared bull was three years old.
He was swift, cunning, strong and bold;
His horns were wide, and his neck was full,
And walked with pride-did long-eared bull.
He bellowed the notes of his challenge call
Till they echoed back from the canyon wall.

One day there chanced to hear him sing,
A waddy who dangled a wicked string,
When he caught a glimpse of the singer's ears
His lips went shut like a pair of shears.
They were both untouched and stood out wide.
He knew that no brand adorned that hide.

He made quite sure that his cinch was tight,
For he knew he was starting a full-grown fight.
He built a loop for a hasty swing
And spurred his horse toward the mountain king.
Away they went like a pair of deer –
The buckaroo and the big long-ear.

He cut down the distance-yard by yard
Till the bull found out he was crowded hard.
He though he'd retreated far enough,
So he whirled about with a charge and snuff,
The cow-horse dodged with a sidewise leap,
The cow-boy threw and he caught him deep.

He caught the bull with a shot-pouch hold,
On the ground the horse and rider rolled.
The puncher saw that it was no use
So he dropped his dallies and turned him loose.
The bull was off like a prairie gale
With a dragging rope and a waving tail.

The cow-boy hung his head in shame-
He had lost his rope, and his horse was lame;
His hands were skinned and his clothes were tom,
He had gone for wool, and had come back shorn.
For if either of them got the wool,
The honors lay with the long-eared bull.

Now a fat old cow-man came one day
On a gentle old flea-bitten gray –
This wise old cow-man had a hunch,
He could humor him in, if he took the bunch.
So he worked them along at an easy pace
And avoided all signs of a fight or race.

He kept well back and circled wide
To corral the bull and to brand his hide.
But just as they got where the brush was thick,
The long-eared bull threw a trump on the trick.
When they got in the open the bull was gone,
And the rest of the bunch was travelling on.

A beardless youngster, lithe and slim,
Was riding one day by the canyon's rim
The happiest youngster in the land,
For just one week he had owned a brand.
He saw the bull and how he smiled,
For the soul of a cow-man was in that child.

He descended the hill with a cheerful heart,
For little he knew of the fight he'd start.
His horse had been ridden some before,
But was hardly wise to the hackamore.
Yet he felt his pulses throb with hope
As he tied the end of his old grass rope.

Well over his saddle horn he humped
And took to the race when the long-ear jumped.
He was one of the kind that never lean back-
He grabbed his horse and he pitched him the slack.

He rapped his flanks with the ringing steel
While the long-eared bull shook a nasty heel.

He built a loop that was big and wide –
He made a throw but the broncho shied,
And sat right back and buried his tail;
Then the button thought he had hooked a whale,
Down went the horse-the youngster fell-
And he used some words that don't print well.

His face was white, but his blood was up,
And he stayed with the fight like a bull-dog pup.
As they buck and bellow, plunge and pull –
The broncho horse and the long eared bull.
For the rope was tied and the saddle big
Was cinched with the old time "Rimmy" rig.

The kid gave a squeal of joy and thanks
As the rope went under the long-ear's flanks.
The horse went bucking off to the right,
To the left the long-ear took his flight.
When they took up the slack the two of them flopped
Right down on their backs and the old rope popped.

The kid was there with an agile spring
His teeth still clinched on his "hoggin' string"
He won by a hair but he did not fail,
For he got his hold on the long-ear's tail.
He tied him down and he swelled with pride
As he run his brand on the glossy hide.

The boy has lived to be old and gray;
He has been successful in every way.
It wasn't by luck-it wasn't by pull –
But the spirit that branded the long-eared bull.
In spite of the fall that ended the ride,
And the whirlwind fight on the mountain side.

The Long Horn Speaks

The old long horn looked at the prize winning steer
And grumbled, "What sort of a thing is this here?
He ain't got no laigs and his body is big,
I sort of suspicion he's crossed with pig.
Now, me! I can run. I can gore. I can kick.
But that feller's too clumsy fer all them tricks.

They're breedin' sech critters and callin' 'em Steers!
Why the horns that he's got ain't as long as my ears.
I cain't figger what he'd have done in my day."
They wouldn't have stuffed me with grain and with hay;
Nor have polished my horns and have fixed up my hoofs
And slept me on beddin' in under the roofs.

Who'd have curried his hide and have fuzzed up his tail?
Not none of them riders that drove the long trail.
They'd have found mighty quick jest how fur he could jump
When they jerked a few doubles of rope of his rump.
And to me it occurs he would not look so slick
With his tail full of burrs and his hide full of ticks.

I wonder jest what that fat feller would think
If he lived on short grass and went miles for a drink,
And wintered out-doors in the sleet and the snow,
He wouldn't look much like he does at the show.
I wouldn't be like him; no, not if I could,
I cain't figger out why they think he's so good.

His little short laigs and his white baby face –
I could finish him off in a fight or a race.
They've his whole fam'ly hist'ry in writin', and still
He ain't fit fer nothin' exceptin' to kill.
And all of them judges that thinks they're so wise,
They look at that critter and give his first prize.

Looking Backward

Do you recollect that country
that you knew in days gone by?
Where the prairie met the sun rise
and the mountains met the sky.
Where you trailed through rugged canons
and on windy mesas wide,
Or you crossed the rollin' prairie
on a long and lonely ride.

How your bits and spurs would jingle.
And the only other sound
Was the creakin' of your saddle
and the hoof beats on the ground.
You was happy in that country,
and among the folks you knew.
Almost any where you landed
there was something you could do.

You would light off of your pony
and you'd stretch and stomp your feet,
When you got that invitation
fer to "Light a spell and eat."
They was faithful to the customs
of the easy goin' west.
You was just a driftin' cow hand
but you was an honored guest.

But things wasn't always funny
in them early days, old pard.
There was times you had no money
and the work was plenty hard.
You was young and you was healthy,
you was never really sick,
But you often travelled limpin'
when a leg got jammed or kicked.

You could tell there had been cattle
in the water that you drank.
And you swallered bugs and wigglers
now and then at some ground tank.
Them big springs in the arroyos,
well, you mostly passed' em by.
They was nice and clear to took at
but full of alkali.

How you rode with Death behind you
when you milled the wild stampeed.
You could feel the lightnin' blind you
as you raced to bend the lead.
How you went out greasy sackin'
in the summer through the hills.
You was shoin', brand in', packin',
cookin', workin' fit to kill.

No there wasn't any wagon
and there wasn't any bunk.
Packed your bed on sweaty hosses.
Man the way them blankets stunk.
Now you tell it with a snicker,
but it griped you then I bet.
Standin' all night in your slicker
'cause your bed was wringin' wet.

Too, you might remember kneel in'
down beside some dying man
While you wrote his last short message
in the book among your brands.
Or you might have seen a quarrel.
Men that had been friends for years.
One or both was dead or dyin'
by the time the smoke was clear.

When you rode up to a bunk house
you was welcomed by the crew,
But you got some recollections
how the bed bugs met you too.
When you went to meet the round up,
you can recollect some day,
When you couldn't find the wagon
or your hosses got away.

Now old hurts come back and pain
you and you've got complainin' toes
That dates back some forty winters
to the time your feet was froze.
And your eyes are weak and tender
from the wind and dust and sun.
That there time you got snow blinded
didn't really help 'em none.

Things are not the way they once was.
There has been a heap of change,
'Mongst the places and the people
since you worked the open range.
In the wide and grassy valleys where
the cattle used to roam,
Now there's irrigatin' ditches,
and there's farms and barns and homes.

There's signs and service stations
where the cattle bedded down.
Where we used to meet the round up
now there's villages and towns.
And the Neon lights is blazin'
where our camp fires glowed so dim.
Concrete bridges span the rivers
where our hosses used to swim.

No you haven't made a fortune, and
    your hair is white. You're old.
But you wouldn't swap your memories;
    not for heaps of shinin' gold.
For whenever you get lonely y
    you put on a big review,
Of the people and the places
    and the hosses that you knew.
You can hear the songs and stories,
    you can see the camp fires blaze,
As you live again the glories of your
    grand old cow boy days.

The Man On The Fence

There's a man that I would speak about,
you see him every where.
He puts out conversations
till he mangles up the air;
No matter what the subject is
his idees are immense.
But he don't go into action.
He's the man that's on the fence.
When the owners ship out cattle
they have all that they can do.
The buyers and the waddies
they are mighty busy too.
Who explains the situation
to a bunch of idle gents?
I needn't tell no body,
it's the feller on the fence.
Who is that can tell you
how a broncho should be rode?
Who is it laughs the loudest
at a feller when he's throwed?
Who tries to be sarcastic
when he makes his wise comments?
Whose pants is full of splinters?
It's the man that's on the fence.

Who is it puts a swagger on
but never gits in trouble?
If he ever gits in danger
who can vanish like a bubble?
Who can tell about a battle
till he holds the crowd plum tense?
Though perhaps he never seen it;
it's the feller on the fence.
Who hollers at old timers
as if they were his pals?

Who has set and spurred the splinters
    from a hundred odd corrals?
Who has spurred the gates and fence rails
    till the boys all know the dents?
It's the man that's always present.
    It's the feller on the fence.
No, he ain't no use fer nothin'
    and he sure does eat a lot.
And he does a heap of talkin'
    that would get a real man shot.
But the outfit tolerates him
    though he ain't worth thirty cents,
Fer he's really right amusin'
    that there feller on the fence.
And it helps an honest waddy
    when he's done his best and failed;
Just to stop and look and listen
    at the feller on the rail.
Fer he knows down in his gizzard,
    if he's got an ounce of sense,
That he's done a durned sight better
    than the man that's on the fence.

The Marking Knife

He sheds his big hat when he gits into town
And his boots aint so good when he's walkin' around.
But there's part of his outfit he don't throwaway.
He's had it fer years and it's with him to stay.
For down in his pocket the rest of his life
The cow puncher carries his old markin' knife.

He could use that sharp blade and beyond all belief.
With nothin' but that he could butcher a beef.
If a slivver got into his hand or his thumb
He would use that old knife blade and out the thing come.
It did his repair work at night in the camps,
He used it fer markin' and whittlin' out clamps.

One time his hoss slipped on a muddy side hill
And he thought that he'd never git clear from that spill.
The hoss lit on his leg and he mighty well knew
By the feel of the stirrup, his foot had gone through.
He held the hoss down by the head with the reins;
He battled and fought, but kept usin' his brains.

He got to the pocket he had in his chaps,
Got his knife, and then cut his off leitigo straps.
When the hoss had got up and he'd saved his own life,
He fixed up the wreck with his old markin' knife.
In plenty of ways any cow puncher found
'Twas a might good thing to have handy around.

With his knife he could all us find sumpthin' to do.
Twas his tool kit, newspaper and radio, too.
He used whenever he worked or he played.
He was allus at home if he had that old blade.
He handles that knife and he dreams of the past,
And he keeps his old markin' knife plum to the last.

The Muley Steer

If there ever was a critter
Put creation out of gear,
And could turn a cow-boy bitter
It's the onery muley steer.
Fer he seems to keep a thinkin'
In his peaked hairy dome,
Has no reg'lar place of drinkin'
Ain't no range where he's at home.
He is always discontented—
Sort of drifts about and mourns,
Seems to drive him plum demented
'Cause he hasn't any horns.

In a herd he's always lurkin'
Somewhere's out along the side.
Always keeps your hoss a workin'
Always makes a feller ride.
On the range, if you pursues him
He takes to it with a rush,
And you're mighty apt to lose him
If he gits into the brush.
Fer the scrub that stops the others,
This onruly critter scorns.
He ain't hampered like his brothers
'Cause he hasn't any horns.

If you jump him on the mountain
There's no tellin' what he'll do;
Fer he has his way of countin,
Sure as one and one is two.
You'll most likely find him hidin'
Up among the highest rocks,
And he scoots right down, a slid in'
On his haunches and his hocks.
When you ketch him he's a puzzle
Fer no prongs his head adorns,
Got to rope him 'round the guzzle
'Cause he hasn't any horns.

I've heard men set up and holler
That he hasn't any sense.
Well, them fellers ort to foller
When he goes around a fence.
He can climb around and blunder
Where you couldn't drive a goat.
He can crawl and burrow under
Like a Poll and Chiny shoat.
If it's wire he'll undo it–
If you build a brake of thorns –
He's the boy can go right through it
'Cause he hasn't any horns.

Don't you think he ain't pugnacious,
Jest because his head is smooth.
He can deal some awful smashes
If you want to know the truth.
And you want to keep your distance
If he starts to bow his neck;
Don't you give him no resistance
If he gits upon the peck.
Fer his head is hard and bony
Look out when he sniffs and warns.
He can sure upset your pony,
If he hasn't any horns.

Yes I know he was created,
But I don't know why or how.
He don't seem to be related
To no other kind of cow.
Fer his mind is plum onsettled,
Though he masters lots of facts,
He keeps men and hosses nettled
By the onery way he acts.
Fer his conscience seems plum pestered
And his skull has ingrown corns
Which same keeps his brain box festered;
'Cause he hasn't any horns.

New Boots

I got my new boots and they fit me jest right.
Of course all the other hands sez they're too tight.
Some sez they're too small, and some sez that they figger
They're shore big enough, but my feet's a heap bigger.

Last night a dumb waddy was springin' a joke,
How I pulled the tape measure so tight that it broke.
I've got the Lumbago—the hands all got cute.
Said I ruint my back pullin' on my new boots.

The boss sez the heels is too high fer his likin'.
Well he shore art to know I don't use boots for hikin'.
They fit me jest perfect. The tops is stitched fine
The bosses boots never was e'kul to mine.

I ordered them boots and I paid the cash down
And they's no better boots in the country around.
I know why them fellers won't let me alone,
When they look at my boots
they're ashamed of their own.

The New Mexico Stray

'Twas a year ago he came from New Mexico;
He was seasoned to the mountains and the plains.
Almost anybody knew that he was a Buckaroo,
By the way he set his hoss and held his reins.

He seemed to onderstand ropin' stock and readin' brands,
And at chasin' hosses he displayed some skill.
But one night the conversation lead to bets and speculation
That a certain hoss could deal him out a spill.

For he wasn't very big, rode a center fire rig,
'Though he seemed to be a likely lookin' lad.
So they cut the boy the hoss jest to see him come across,
For they wanted to discover what he had.

Well, the stranger placed his leather safely on the hoss's weathers,
And he stepped right up aboard him with a grin;
Oh the crowd was sure in luck when the hoss began to buck,
For they tangled in the air to beat the wind.

Yes, old hoss-he humped and curled,
Then went up, came down and whirled,
On a piece of ground no bigger than a dime.
But the stranger kept a straddle of his center-fire saddle,
And his quirt and spurs was workin' over time.

Well that made us all decide that perhaps the boy could ride—
We were sorry when we found he could not stay.
He was with us half a year, and we wish he still was here,
But some outfit has a cow-boy anyway.

And we'll meet again some day in some outfit far away,
When I go to meet the round-up with my string.
He'll come joggin' in astraddle of his center-fire saddle,
With his hook-down spurs that have the wicked ring –

Then we'll stop and have a smoke
and we'll gossip and we'll joke,
'Bout the places and the people that we know;
For, I'll have you onderstand that the average cattle hand,
Don't forget the times and friends of long ago.

Old And Foxy

It is likely he was in the drive
among the other stock,
Till he got a chance to sneak away
and hide behind a rock.
He had his idee figgered out.
He'd planned it in advance,
And he wasn't slow about it
when he saw he had a chance.

He's been playin' tag with cow boys
since the day that he was born.
Every year that he could dodge 'em
meant a wrinkle on his horn.
When the round up is a workin'
he will watch 'em for a week.
He comes down at night fer water,
then goes back up on the peak.

I'll bet there's times that critter
  sorter squints his eyes and smiles.
He jest walks around some boulders
  while they're ridin' miles and miles.
He's afraid of men and hosses,
  he has seen 'em come and go.
He stays up in the pinnacles
  and watches things below.

By the time some rider climbs the hill
  and gets where he was at,
He's got plum off from that mountain
  and he's half accrost the flat.
People say old steers git foxy.
  That is what I have been told.
But I reckon that's the only kind
  that lives to git so old.

Well, he is livin' in the hills
  long after gentle stock
Has been hung up in the packin' house
  and chopped up on the block.
It may be learned or natural,
  he's a smart one just the same.
And you got to give him credit
  every time he beats the game.

The Old Cow Pony

Hello there old feller. I'm speakin' to you.
No need to look at me the way that you do.
When we git acquainted I think you will find,
I know quite a bit about you and your kind.

With your wicked bright eyes and your tough shaggy coat,
And about as sure footed and tough as a goat.
You was chuck full of Hell from your nose to your tail.
You came North with the herds when they drove the long trail.

Through the heat and the dust when the goin' was hard
Out in the dim star light you held the lone guard.
On the dark stormy night when the herd would stampede,
You carried the riders that "Bended the lead."

You was never a thing to be petted or trusted.
Most every old cow poke has bones that you busted.
But them old boys swear by you. You bet they all do.
And they'd like to build statues to hosses like you.

Old Frosty

Old Frosty was a round up cook
  as cranky as a grizzly bear.
Knowed all the answers in the book
  besides a few that wasn't there
When first we felt the breath of Spring
  and coyotes had a cheerful howl.
When other folks began to sing
  old Frosty started in to growl
He didn't like the summer crew.
  He called 'em nothin' to admire.
He said not one among 'em knew
  the way to set a wagon tire.
And when they tried to tell him news,
  or let him in on some big scheme,
He'd tell 'em go and nail some shoes
  onto the old chuck wagon team.

He'd clean the wagon spick and span
  and cuss because we'd lost some bowls.
I mind one time he kicked a man that
  used his pots to boil some clothes.

He always cussed the winter hands
    before he got his wagon packed
Because they loand out pots and pans
    and somehow failed to get 'em back.

They'd start him to the general store
    to fill his list and get his load.
He answered short and even swore
    if someone stopped him on the road.
But at the store I'll have to say
    his manner was polite and pleasant.
For every time he drove away
    he got tobacker for a present.

One time two punchers short on brains
    with spurs a rattlin' on their heels
Tied up their hosses by the reins
    to Frosty's hind chuck wagon wheels.
Old Frosty grabbed an empty sack
    and brushed them hosses in the face.
They broke the reins when they set back
    and Frosty chunked 'em off the place.

Them punchers swore they'd whip a cook
    and their intentions was all right
But Frosty grabbed his old pot hook
    and them two fellers lost a fight.
He'd tell us boys to bring some wood
    when we come into camp at night.
That didn't do a bit of good.
    All we brought was our appetite.
Him and the wranglers always fit,
    because he kept 'em doin' chores.
And every time a wrangler quit
    it always made the boss plum sore.
We wondered why they kept the cuss.
    We hated him with all our souls
And reckoned someday one of us
    would have to shoot him full of holes.

His face it was no maiden's dream;
    but Frosty always did his part.
He'd pull a big load with a team that
    other fellers couldn't start.
The meals he cooked was plenty good.
    I think sometimes I taste 'em yet.
We often wondered how he could
    when mud was deep and wood was wet.

He wanted to be let alone,
    he didn't care to laugh or joke;
But he could set a broken bone
    or doctor up a sick cow poke.
He never did throw off or shirk
    he kept us free from mounted tramps.
The round up boss he run the work
    and let Old Frosty run the camps.

And then one spring he failed to show.
    The boss he waited hoped and trusted
The hands allowed that mebbyso
    Old Frosty got so mad he busted.
They got a man to take his place
    that had a better disposition
He had a cheerful way and face
    but only half as much ambition.

He was fair to middlin' cook.
    The bosses reckoned he was good.
But anything he undertook
    he done just half what Frosty could.
Old Frosty can't be livin' now.
    He's up above or down below,
But I will gamble anyhow
    that where he's at he runs the show.

The Old Night Hawk

I am up tonight in the pinnacles bold,
Where the rim rock towers high;
Where the air is clear, and the wind blows cold,
And there's only the horses and I.
The desert swims like a silver sea
In the light of the big full moon,
And strong and clear there comes to me
The lilt of the first guard's tune.

The fire at camp is burning bright –
Cook's got more wood than he needs.
They'll be telling some awful tales tonight
Of races and big stampedes.
I'm gettin' too old fer that line of talk –
The desperaders they've knowed,
Their wonderful ways to of handle stock,
And the fellers they've seen git throwed.

I guess I'm a dog that has had his day,
Though I still am quick and strong;
But my hair and my beard have both turned gray,
And I reckon I've lived too long.
None of 'em know me but that old cook, Ed,
And never a word he'll say –
My story will stick in his old gray head
Till the break of the judgment day.

What's that I see that's a walkin' fast?
It's a hoss a slippin' through!
He's a tryin' to make it out through the pass –
Come mighty near doin' it too.
Git back there, what are you tryin' to do?
You hadn't a chance to bolt!
Old boy I was wranglin' a bunch like you
Before you was even a colt.

It's later now, the guard has changed;
One voice is clear and strong.
He's singin' a tune of the old time range –
I always did like that song.
It takes me back to when I was young
And the memories came through my head
Of the times I have heard the old song sung,
By voices now long since dead.

I have traveled better than half my trail,
I'm well down the further slope.
I've seen all my dreams and ambitions fail
And memory replaces hope.
It must be true, fer I've heard it said,
It's only the good die young.
The tough old cusses like me and Ed
Must stay till the last dog's hung.

I used to shrink when I thought of the Past
And some of the things I've known.
I took to drink, bur now at last,
I'd far rather be alone.
It's strange how quick a night goes by,
Fir I live in the days of old.
Up here where there's only the horses and I –
Up in the pinnacles bold.

The two short years when I ceased to roam,
And I lived a contented life.
Then trouble came and I left my home,
And I never have heard of my wife.
The years I spent in a prison cell
When I went by another name;
For life is a mixture of Heaven and Hell –
To a feller that plays the game.

They'd better layoff of that wrangler kid –
They've give him about enough.
He looks like a pardner of mine once did.
He's the kind that a man can't bluff.
They'll find that they are making a big mistake
If they once git him over het;
And they'll give him as good as an even break,
Or I'm taken' a hand, you bet!

Look, there in the East is the mornin' star!
It shines with a firey glow,
Till it looks like the end of a big cigar,
But it hasn't got far to go.
Just like the people that make a flash –
They don't stand much of a run –
Come bustin in with a sweep and dash,
When most of the work is done.

I can see the East is gettin' gray –
I'll gather the hosses soon;
And faint from the valley far away
Comes the drone of the last guard's tune.
Yes, life is just like the night-herd's song,
As the long years come and go –
You start with a swing that is free and strong,
And finish up tired and slow.

I reckon the hosses all are here –
I can see that "T-bar" blue,
And the buckskin hoss with the one split ear;
I've got 'em all. Ninety two.
Just listen to how they roll the rocks –
These sure are rough old trails;
But then, if they can't slide down on their hocks
They can coast along on their tails.

The Wrangler Kid, he's out with his rope,
He hardly misses a throw.
Will he make a cow hand? I should hope,
If they give him half a show.
They're throwin' the rope corral around,
The hosses crowd in like sheep.
I reckon I'll swaller my breakfast down
And try to furgit and sleep.

Yes, I've lived my life and I've took a chance,
Regardless of law or vow.
I've played the game, and I've had my dance,
And I'm payin' the fiddler now.

(Borein)

The Old Time Christmas

I liked the way we used to do,
  when cattle was plenty and folks was few.
The people gathered frum far and near, and
  they barbacued a big fat steer.
The kids tried stayin' awake because,
  they reckoned they might ketch Santa Claus.
Next mornin' you'd wake 'em up to see,
  what he'd been and put on the Christmas tree.

It was Christmas then fer the rich and pore,
  and every ranch was an open door.
The waddy that came on a company hoss
  was treated the same as the owner and boss.
Nobody seemed to have a care,
  you was in among friends or you wasn't there.
For every feller in them days knew
  to behave hisself as a man should do.

Some had new boots, which they'd shore admire
when they warmed their feet in front of there.
And the wimmin folks had new clothes too,
    but not like the wimmin of these days do.
Some times a drifter came riding in,
    some feller that never was seen agin.
And each Christmas day as the years went
    on we used to wonder where they'd gone.

I like to recall the Christmas night.
    The tops of the mountains capped with white.
The stars so bright they seemed to blaze,
    and the foothills swum in a silver haze.
Them good old days is past and gone.
    The time and the world and the change goes on.
And you cain't do things like you used to do
    when cattle was plenty and folks was few.

The Old West

When folks think of the places and times they like best,
That's when most old timers remember the west.
The West in the days it was really immense.
When you travelled for miles without findin a fence.

There was not many churches and not many schools.
There was no regulations and mighty few rules.
It come 'bout as near as a country could be
To what you might call the real land of the free.

There was nobody asked where you got what you owned.
They minded their business and let you alone.
If you made a success or you wound up in ruin,
They figgered you'd ort to know what you was doin'!

You bought your own chips and you played your own game.
No one but yourself was to praise or to blame.
If you got into trouble, nobody horned in.
You could run or die fightin' or mebby so win.

You could fight with a club, you could shoot or throw rocks.
You could die in your moccaisons, boots, or your sock.
Nobody advised you out in the Old West.
You did things the way you could do 'em the best.

Just where a man come from, them folks didn't care.
When he wanted to leave that was his own affair.
On the ranches and ranges, in old Western towns,
If a feller was useful they kept him around.

There was now and then fellers got lynched by a mob.
But not often a man that was holdin' a job.
You could deal with a bad man in case that you knew it
There was plenty to do and not many to do it.

So if the survivor could be of some use.
The crowd was in favor of turnin' him loose.
They wanted good men but they wanted still more.
They wanted to know what a man was good for.

Now a law man he had to be quick on the draw.
With brains in his head and with sand in his craw.
A lot of the people he handled was tough
And an officer didn't get far on a bluff.

If there's stuff to be moved or there's goods to be hauled,
Well, somebody wanted a freighter, that's all.
There was cattle by thousands a runnin' wild loose
And plenty of work for some real buckaroos.

And so many young horses; I'm tellin' you mister,
Them folks almost worshipped a real broncho twister.
A man that could count to a hundred could teach,
And any old fool that could holler could preach.

What brand of religion? Them folks didn't mind.
He could have a religion of most any kind.
A catholic or protestant, yes either one.
He could dance with the Injuns and worship the Sun.

Them citizens wasn't compelled to believe it.
You could listen or not. You could take it or leave it.
He might be a bachelor or have several wives.
That didn't mean no thin' in other folks' lives.

No one in the settlement cared what he did
If he fed his own women and raised his own kids.
He could pray to Mohammed to salvage his soul.
He could build him a shrine or a tall totem pole.

It seemed like in them days that nobody worried
Nobody was idle but nobody hurried.
Some of ' em was good and some of 'em was bad.
They did what they could with the chances they had.

Yes that is the way they did things in the west,
And that was the reason we liked it the best.
It come 'bout as near as a country could be,
To what you might call the real land of the free.

Our Boss

He started young and he drifted far
The owner out at the Diamond-Bar.
He has cattle grazing on many a hill,
But down in his heart he's a cow-boy still.

Though other owners put on airs,
It's little for style that our boss cares;
He wears his boots and his leather chaps,
And everybody calls him "Tap."

He bandies jokes and exchanges news,
As he rides the range with his buckaroos;
He sits his horse with a careless grace,
And rides at a stockman's jogging pace.

But the horses he rides all come of a breed
That are bred for mettle and built for speed.
The thing that he really most enjoys
Is a horse round-up with a bunch of boys.

It's then he rides at a pace that kills,
Through the open flats and the rugged hills;
With spurs set close and with flying reins –
Like he rode when a boy on the Texas plains.

Or else, when he jumps big mountain steers,
That have dodged the round-up for several years –
Down comes his rope, and away they dash,
While the hoof-beats ring and the cedars crash,
Till the bellowing steer on the mountain side,
Proclaims the fact that he's roped and tied.

I have seen him riding at racing speed –
Singing in front of a mad Stampede –
As calmly as most old gentlemen do,
When sitting at church in a rented pew.

If he did retire and settle down
He would waste away in the sheltered town
Where he couldn't hear the cattle bawl,
The horses neigh, and the coyote's call.
He was raised on the range, and there he stayed –
One of the boys of the old brigade.

The Panther Track*

It was way out at a water hole
a hoss come in to drink.
You and your partner ketched him,
and it made you look and think.
The bridle reins was draggin',
he'd a saddle on his back,
And across that empty saddle
was a fresh made panther track.

Well, there wasn't no denyin'
that the rider had been throwed.
But he shore left there a tryin'
that was mighty plainly showed.
Even if he was caught nappin'
and a settin' sorter slack,
He went out of there a tryin'
that's what made the panther track.

You looked in the saddle blankets
fer a sign of leaves or brush.
Might have run in some rough country,
and got dragged off in the rush.
There was nothin' in the blankets
and the rope was tied up tight,
And the pony wasn't spur marked;
it was sorter strange all right.

* (A spur mark across a saddle.)

So he wasn't chasin' nothin',
and the pony hadn't bucked,
It shore struck you mighty funny
he had meet up with bad luck.
But the man had lost his saddle
and the hoss had slipped his pack,
That was wrote as plain as day light,
in that fresh made panther track.

Well, you rode up the hog back
and you searched the whole sky line.
Fer a smoke or any signal
you could foller fer a sign.
And his hoss was smart and gentle,
follered right up on the slack,
While you wondered why that feller
ever made that panther track.

You back tracked until you found him.
He was layin' mighty still.
Ants all over and around him,
where the trail come off the hill.
Yes, you sent word to his outfit
and they took his body back.
But nobody knows the reason
why he made that panther track.

The Parada Shark

Was you ever out herdin' the "Prather,"
On a beautiful clear summer day,
When the cattle all stayed right together,
And none of ' em wanted to stray?
With yer pardner and one other feller –
The grass was so thick and so–
The breeze was so soothin' and meller,
And you'd just changed your clothes and felt clean?

You was feeling plum elegant mental,
An' had et a big dinner beside,
An' yer half-broken hoss was so gentle
He was like a pet pony to ride.
An' the clouds was so white they was gleamin'
While a-driftin' around in the sky,
An' you watched 'em an, got sort 0' dreamin',
There was pictures up there, betcher eye!

A castle that had a big steeple,
A bird that had beautiful wings,
An' animals, houses an' people –
An' hoi jest a whole lot of things!
An' a plum– bigger –
In wonderful loose fittin' clothes;
She shore had a mighty fine figger –
You sort of admired her pose.

You felt like the world was "Sta bueno,"
Or a little bit better than that;
Then you thought you were on a volcano,
An' you flew out from under your hat.
You grabbed for the lady an' castle.
But somehow yer arms didn't hit,
An' you found you had started to wrestle
With a greasewood that growed where you lit.

The boys chased yer hoss till they ketched him—
You was feelin' all shook up an' cheap.
They'd a plenty to say when they fetched him,
Bout watchin' you goin' to sleep.
Did you ever let sech a thing happen—
I'm willin' to gamble you did—
Let your hoss go to sleep an' be nappin',
And get bucked off-just like a kid?

And wake up all dusty and shakin'—
But then that's the way with most dreams;
Most folks gits a sudden awakin'—
Things ain't always jest what they seems.

The Pet Hoss

I once rode a pet hoss, as onery a scamp
As ever tormented a ranch or a camp.
An old winter hoss and I needn't explain,
He got his bad habits from bein' fed grain.
He would open a gate and git into a shed,
He would tear open grain sacks or paw up a bed.
He would bust up a bucket or batter a pan
Why he never got killed I jest caint onderstand.

When ridin' along, if you didn't go fast
He would root at the bit and go grabbin' fer grass.
If you doubled yore rope up and welted his hide
He would flinch and he'd beg till it looked like he cried.
He was like lots of people. Go nosin' about
Till he got into trouble, then try to beg out.
If you whipped him he'd jump and light in the same tracks
If you spurred him he'd groan and jest hump up his back.

But boy he was tough beyond question or doubt.
He took that old jog trot and never wore out.
And jump out a critter – Good Lord how he'd go.
He would take you right to him and give you a throw.
He didn't care how many loops that you spilt,
He stayed right at their tail till another was built.
He knowed how to widen and how to set back,
When you'd tied you could call him, he'd step up and slack.

Another thing too that may seem sort of strange,
You could walk up and ketch him, turned loose on the range.
He helped me one day when I'd made a hard run
With a long ride ahead, which I shouldn't have done.
The hoss I was rid in' was draggin' his feet,
And the dust devils danced in a shimmer of heat.
I spotted some hosses. They let me git nigh.
In the heat waves they looked 'bout a dozen feet high.

They all trotted off, that is all except one,
There stood the old pet hoss, the son of a gun.
The hoss I was on couldn't make a good lope
And the pet hoss would run if I took down my rope.
He had been runnin' out since along in the spring,
But I got him on foot, with an old hoggin' string.
Yes a pet hoss is onery and mean, that's a cinch
But they're mighty durned handy sometimes in a pinch.

Pullin' Bog

When the water gits thick and the mud sorter thin.
When the cows come to drink and the weak ones slides in;
And once a pore critter gits down in a bog,
She lays there as dead as a watersoaked log.

You offer 'em help and they won't ev'n try.
They are not only willin' but wantin' to die.
And the buzzards they gether and circle around,
They are always on hand when a critter gits down.

You pull and you waller and haul her around
Till you finally git her out onto dry ground.
When you git her pulled out by the horns or the neck,
She aint a bit thankful, but goes on the peck.

She lowers her horns and she charges right in.
But she's mostly so weak that she falls down ag'in.
But there's people you've helped that have acted the same;
So generally speakin', a cow aint to blame.

Pullin' Leather

Yes, a cow boy has his troubles,
and he shore is out of luck,
Out a dozen miles from nowheres
and his hoss begins to buck.
And he picks a place to practice
on some mighty ugly ground,
For you'd land amongst the cactus
if he ever got you down.

So you aim to keep a straddle
and you'll ride him if you can,
'Elst they'll be a dehorned saddle,
or they'll be a one armed man.
You don't look like much vaquero,
he is floppin' yore shirt tails.
You have lost yore old sombrero
and you've broke some finger nails.

People say that pullin' leather
don't show ridin' skill. That's true.
But you'd like to stick together
till the argyment is through.
When yo're a slippin' and a slidin',
you'll admit at all events
If it doesn't show good ridin'
that it shows a heap of sense.

When yo're throwed it ain't so pleasant
with a dozen miles to walk.
No there ain't nobody present,
and the hoss of course cain't talk.
You are hangin' on and prayin'.
You ain't makin' no grand stand.
You jest aim to keep a stayin'
and you'll do the best you can.

Puttin' On A Show

This boy is sure good and he takes lots of pride
In showin' the others how well he can ride.
He ain't only contented with "Ridin' him Slick."
He has pitched him the slack and he's doin' some tricks.

He sets right straight up and he looks at his friends.
He is holdin' his moustache and twistin' the ends.
If you've got an idee that is easy to do,
Try it out when a hoss starts to buckin' with you.

You will find your hand flyin' all over the place,
And it's luck if you don't hit yourself in the face.
A buckin' hoss don't look so bad to the gents
That are on gentle hosses or roost on the fence.

But the man that can ride him and finish on top,
And twist his moustache is a hard one to stop.
We don't like a feller that shows off, but still,
He sure has a right to be proud of his skill.

The Race For The Wagon

The cook is at work with his pots and pans.
In sight of the wagon, this bunch of hands
Is racin' to see who'll be first in,
There aint no stakes but they ride to win.
We know it's a thing that was often done;
It didn't mean nothin, just cow boy fun.
And a gallop does rest a man a lot
That has rode fer miles at a walk or trot.

The cook keeps on a mixin' his dough,
He got used to them races years ago,
And the average old time round up cook
Would be too stubborn to even look.
He has work of his own that he has to do
If the others can play they're welcome to.
He bakes the biscuits and fries the meat
To be ready in time fer the hands to eat.

The sun shines bright on the flats and hills,
The summer day is warm and still.
The smoke goes straight toward the clear blue sky –
Not even a clowd is driftin' by.
There's many an old time buckaroo
Who's ridin' days are long since through,
Who would like to be there and would shore be prowd
To race for the wagon along with the crowd.

Rain

It's sumpthin' a feller caint hardly explain
The way that a cow puncher feels about rain.
It makes the feed grow and it fills up the tanks,
And generally speakin' he'd orta give thanks.
He wakes up some night when the rain hits his bed
And pulls the tarpolian up over his head.
It's warm when it rains and he gits overhet
And he lays there all night in a miserable sweat.

He wakes up next mornin', his boots is all soaked
Jest laugh that one off if you think it's a joke.
He pulls at the lugs and he stomps and he knocks
Till he drives both his feet through the toes of his socks.
He gits his boots on but you know how it feels;
No toes in his socks and them wrinkled up heels.
When he goes to ketch out it ain't no easy trick
With a rope that is wet and as stiff as a stick.

He dabs for his hoss and he makes a good snare
But the hoss downs his head and backs right out from there.
Fer a cow pony knows you caint tighten a loop
When you ketch with a rope that's as stiff as a hoop.
When he gits saddled up he must climb up and ride
And that. wets the last dry spot he had on his hide.
The hoss starts to buck but that cow boy is set
Fer a man's hard to throw when his saddle is wet.

All day he keeps ridin' the flats and the hills,
A slippin' and slidin' and likely he spills.
When he gits into camp he must stand up to eat,
And his clothes is all wet from his head to his feet.
He stands 'round the fire, he cusses and smokes,
Fer he hates to git into a bed that's all soaked.
But his slicker's wet through fer it's old any way,
And there's mighty few slickers turns water all day.

And while he turns in, and as strange as it seems
He goes off to sleep and he sweats and he steams.
Next mornin' it's clear and the wind's blow in' sharp
He shivers and crawls out from under his tarp.
By the time he eats breakfast he's feelin' all right
And his bed will dry out by a couple more nights.
But the old saddle blankets are still cold and wet,
And the hoss humps his back and looks wicked you bet.

Old cow boy is tired, he's stiff and he's sore,
He's had lots of trouble, he don't want no more.
So he takes that old pony and leads him around
Till he gits his back warm and the saddle sets down.
Fer the man that's been rained on two nights and a day,
Ain't lookin' fer trouble; he ain't built that way.
He wants feed and water but let me explain,
A waddy ain't comf'tble out in the rain.

The Rifle

You can talk of the flag that our ancestors bore,
But what backed it up when they started to war?
They had orators, statesmen, intelligent men,
Who did wonderful things with the treaty and pen;
But let me express my opinion right here,
It was mostly the rifle, that tamed the frontier.

When a settler and family moved into the woods,
It was little they had, either money or goods.
What protected their home in that desolate spot?
What furnished the meat that they cooked in the pot?
What brought in the hides of the bear and the deer?
That old fashioned rifle, that tamed the frontier.

Yes, history can tell you the part that she played
When they fought for their lives at some rude barricade.
When the fierce painted warriors charged with a yell,
With knives and with hatchets, like demons from Hell,
Right back to their war cry, rang, deadly and clear,
The voice of the rifle, that tamed the frontier.

Each time foreign soldiers set foot on our soil,
And the farmers and tradesmen abandoned their toil,
Their soldiers and officers soon learned to fear,
The voice of that rifle, that tamed the frontier.

When the ox wagons travelled the mountains and plains,
Through the heat and the dust; through the snows and the rains;
No law to protect them, they went without fear.
They carried the rifle that tamed the frontier.

When the renegades cornered some lone grizzled trapper,
They had trouble in handling that crafty old scrapper.
The battle light, gleamed in his faded hard eye.
When he laid the gray whiskers, just under his ear,
On the stock of the rifle, that tamed the frontier.

When the gangs of tough outlaws sprang up in the west
And they got to the place they were really a pest;
The citizens gathered, and formed a committee,
Who wasted no time, and who wasted no pity.
The old vigilanties put things in the clear.
With the rope and the rifle, they tamed the frontier.

At last the breach loader arrived on the scene.
The cow boy's short rifle. The trooper's "Carbeen."
When the range wars were gripping men body and soul,
And some boy was corralled at a lone water hole;
Outnumbered, surrounded, he sold his life dear,
With the cow boy's rifle, that tamed the frontier.

When the grizzly was gone and the Indian tame,
And the buffalo had vanished, the scatter gun came.
And gone to his rest was the grim pioneer,
And the old fashioned rifle, that tamed the frontier.

But he left us a heritage none can deny.
Our cause or our country should neither one die.
In times of depression, in moments of doubt.
If there's treason within, if there's foemen without,
Let them listen to reason, or else, let them hear,
The voice of the rifle, that tamed the frontier.

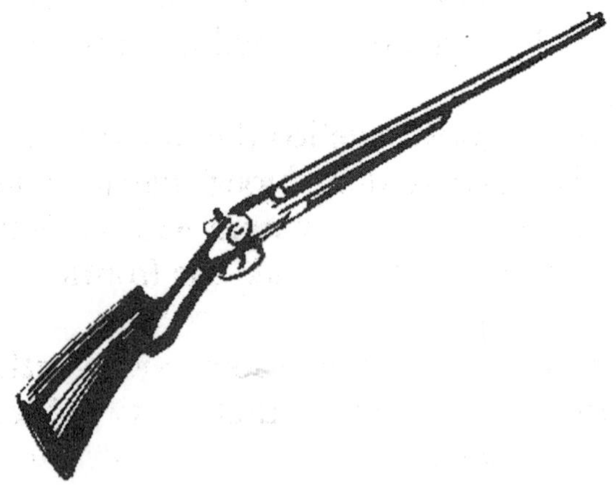

The Rope Corral

Remember when you saddled up
jest shortly after dawn?
I reckon that you ain't forgot it Pal.
When the boys was busy
ketchin' out and throwin' saddles on,
And the hosses in the old time rope corral.

You ask me if that single strand
would hold 'em? Well I hope.
They was foxy, they was skittish, but you bet,
They'd been trained when they was broken
not to run against a rope,
In a way they didn't very soon forget.

They would crowd and duck and scramble,
and you'd have to watch around,
Till you got a chance to "dab" it on your hoss.
Then they'd let one rope go slack
until it rested on the ground.
It was easy then to lead him out across.

Yes the trick was very simple,and was very clever too;
But the whole affair can easy be explained.
You can nearly always figger
what a man or hoss will do,
If you know the way
that he was raised and trained.

The Running Iron

I have kept this running iron
    that an old friend handed me.
Many weary miles it travelled
    underneath a cow boy's knee.
Through the sun and rain of summer,
    through the winter's cold and snow,
It was fastened to his saddle
    everywhere he chanced to go.

It has been upon a night horse.
    It was flung beneath a shed.
And it layout in the starlight,
    on the saddle by his bed.
Yes, you know without my saying,
    it was made to run a brand,
But it broke a trail through cactus,
    out upon the desert sand.

It's been behind a long ear
    while they made the gravel fly,
Racing through the rocks and timber
    for a place to catch and tie.
It would knock out heavy gravel
    that got in a horse's feet,
And for finishing a rattler
    it was mighty hard to beat.

You can see without half trying
    that this implement would hurt.
It would help subdue a broncho
    if you didn't have a quirt.
I don't say he hunted trouble,
    but I intimate he might
Just have used this running iron
    when it eqalized a fight.

Yes it rode upon his saddle
    through the cold and through the heat.
It's been held above the embers
    while he grilled a piece of meat.
For its owner was a cow boy,
    by which reason I suppose,
There's a lot of little secrets
    that this running iron knows.

Sidin' His Dad

Now can't you remember when you was a lad
And you started out ridin' along with your Dad.
You first rode behind him. How awkward you felt,
When you grabbed at the saddle or hung to his belt.

Then you rode an old gentle hoss barebacked, alone,
Till at last you'd a saddle and hoss of your own
And you was so tickled and happy inside,
You was ready to bust, you was so full of pride.

You think of it now lookin' back through the years.
That was long long ago, but the memory is clear.
It is likely your father has gone to his rest,
And the saddle and pony, of course they "went west."

And the wide open country you used to admire,
Is dotted with houses or shut in with wire.
The motor cars crowded the hosses away.
They do in an hour what took you a day.

There was years of hard work, and a lot of hard rides,
And many a range pal you travelled beside.
But never a thrill like when you were a lad,
And you rode your first saddle, 'longside of your Dad.

The Silk Shirt

You recollect that pink silk shirt
you bought so long ago,
The time us boys went into town
to see the rodeo.
The second day you had it,
it begun to show the dirt.
When you wore it after sun down
you would git so cold you hurt.

But the first time that we branded,
well, it didn't look so new:
It appeared plum second handed;
tore and smeared with blood and goo.
Next day, well, you jumped some hosses
and you had to make a ride,
When you took 'em off the mesa
and come down the mountain side.

When they took you through the cedars,
why yore shirt begun to tear.
By the time you hit the slide rock
jest a part of it was there.
But the thing was tore to ribbons,
and yore hide was scratched, oh gosh!
When you once got through the cat claw
that was growin' in the wash.

At the old home ranch that evenin'
you was settin' on a rail.
You still had the cuffs and collar
and a portion of the tail.
So you put yore old brush jumper on.
'Twas full of sweat and dirt.
But 'twas built to hold a cow boy
better than a pink silk shirt.

The Stage Driver

The man that drove the stage coach
didn't have no smooth paved road.
He got all kinds of weather,
and sometimes a heavy load.
The road was just some wheel tracks
among the rocks and sand;
He'd a team of half broke hosses
and he drove 'em four in hand.

When once they got him started
he was really on his own.
There wasn't no highway patrol
nor any telephone.
He looked to his team and harness,
buckled on his old six gun,
'Cause most any thing could happen
'fore he finished up his run.

Them old drivers might be faulty
but they shore was fust class hands.
You would find 'em plenty salty
and their craw was full of sand.
They wasn't picked fer beauty
and they wasn't picked fer style.
They picked 'em out fer all them things
that makes a man wuth while.

He had responsibility.
He had his trip to make.
He had the mail sack,
and the lives of passengers at stake.
In all the history of the West,
he has his place and page;
For everybody must respect the man
that drove the stage.

The Stampede

The afterglow fades and the daylight is failing,
Deep gloom settles over the valley so wide;
The slow moving column of cattle goes trailing,
The men that were silent, now sing as they ride.
For the cattle are nervous-they break and they rally;
They've been getting worse since the set of the sun.
They're used to the mountains, they fear the wide valley;
They're off of their range and they're ready to run.

The leaders break back, and the herd ceases drifting;
The cordon of riders looks pitifully thin
For the army of steers that are surging and shifting,
But the boys from the mountains are holding them in.
The horses are ready and up on their mettle,
They know what it means, they're giving them room.
But slowly the herd is beginning to settle—
The cow-boys are bedding them down in the gloom.

"Oh beat the drum lowly and play the fife slowly."
Two cow-punchers sing as they meet and turn back.
One jolly vacquero sings "Billy Vaniero."
Another one sings of the "The Tumble Down Shack."
You hear the old tune, with its sad wailing minor,
Of "Oh Bury Me Not on the Lone Prairie."
While faint from the distance, but clearer and finer
Rings out the old melody "Mother Machree."

The hours drag on and the cattle are sleeping.
Except for the singing it's silent as death.
Through the yuccas and greasewood
the night wind comes creeping,
So softly you scarce hear the sound of its breath.
A gopher hole does it-a horse makes a blunder—
He recovers himself but he snorts as he leaps.
The cattle are off with a rumble like thunder
And over the valley the avalanche sweeps.

Race! Race for the front, every man that's behind them.
Get out on the point and help mill the stampede.
The holes and brush and the ditches, don't mind them
And ride for your life if you're caught in the lead.

There's tons upon tons in their onrushing forces,
These wild mountain cattle unruly and large.
They're bigger than mules and they're stronger than horses,
And swift in their rush as a cavalry charge.
The well-seasoned riders are not a bit tardy—
The cattle are quick but the men are the same.
On tough mountain horses, sure-footed and hardy,
The cow-boys are taking a stack in the game.

They're skillful and willing, they start the herd milling;
They circle around them, they sing and they call.
The mad pace grows slower, the dust clouds sink lower;
At last they stop running; They've starting to bawl.
They halt and start backing; they jam-they are packing
They stop. They are standing all silent and still!
Don't crowd them! Be steady! Keep wide but be ready.
They may settle down, but they're likely to spill.

A steer snuffs and bellows; two dare-devil fellows
Are caught in the front, but they're off at full speed.
You can hear them both singing-their voices are ringing—
Grim death's at their heels but they're crowding the lead.
The herd starts to scatter, but that doesn't matter;
It's every one now to do what he thinks best.
In front or behind them, they race where they find them;
They do what they can and turn over the rest.

At last the light comes and the stars have all faded,
The bleary-eyed riders look haggard and drawn.
Their strong mountain horses are weary and jaded
But slowly they gather the herd in the dawn.
On comes the "Remuda" and every one changes;
They breakfast in relays — they're back on their way.
It's little they worry — these boys of the ranges.
It's just what a cow-puncher calls a long day.

They are every one used to that sort of a battle.
It's just a hard night; they're glad it is gone.
It's nothing, so long as they don't lose their cattle,
And every one's there when they meet in the dawn.

Stan*

Saint Peter stood at the Golden Gate
Givin' the crowd the works.
The people was there from ev'ry state,
Missourians, Jews and Turks.
They were all in line and things went fine
Till the system got upset.
Up rode a man by the name of Stan
From the *Brewery Gulch Gazette.*

"Git this through yore head," Saint Peter said,
"So fur yore the only one
That has dast come here in his ridin' gear
On a onery wall eyed dunn.
You said yore a dude, but yore rough and rude,
And I'd have you onderstand,
You have got the walk, the way and the talk,
Of a regular old rough hand.

"You ain't allowed in the Gospel crowd.
One reason you caint get through,
We've got some folks don't like yore jokes,
From the W.C.T.U.
Yore a gain' to clear right out from here,
Both you and that wall eyed brute.
I'm a shippin' you South to the Parrninint drouth.
Git into that left hand chute!"

---

* Refers to Stan Adler, editor of the *Brewery Gulch Gazette* in Bisbee, Arizona.

Stan raked the dunn, and the son of a gun
Raired straight as a dyin' whale.
When he hit the ground his head come down
And he shore did swaller his tail.
Stan waved his hat and fanned his fat
And give' em the cow boy yell.
And you art to have heered how the Devil cheered
As he stood on the gates of Hell.

'Twas a clever trick and he worked it slick.
They found it out too late.
He steered the wreck with a spur in his neck,
Right in through the open gate.
Saints shuffled their feet on the golden street
When they ran behind telephone poles.
Stan was first to ride plum high and wide
Through the city of ransomed souls.

There could nothin' out run that wall eyed dunn;
They went through the town right quick.
He last was seen in the pasters green
A head in' right up the crick.
Old Soloman Wise of the sportin' guys,
Went over and cashed a bet.
He had bet on the man by the name of Stan,
From the *Brewery Gulch Gazette.*

Swimmin' The Herd

The river is up, but then the boss
Has done give powders' to swim across.
The remuda comes with the wrangler kid,
He pulls up his belt and pulls down his lid.
They go right in and the wrangler hangs
To his hoss's tail or the saddle whangs.

The lead they foller, jest watch 'em string
And into the stream rides the point and swing.
But they double back and they mill around
And a lot of the herd is due to drownd.
Come on! some man of the bull dog breed,
Git into that circle and start a lead.

A thing like that ain't nice to meet
Them crowd in' bodies and treadin' feet—
You must git right in till you smell their breath
And you're stickin' yore face in the jaws of death.
But into the mill goes a buckaroo,
A dead game cow boy through and through.

There isn't so much to see at that.
The cattle's heads and a Stetson hat
And a floatin' mane in the churnin' strife
There a game old cow hoss fights for life.
Till he starts a lead and they're swinimin' clear
And even the hard old riders cheer.

And the whole durned world can lift their hat
To a feller that's cheered by a crowd like that.
And now the cattle are gain' fine
A dozen abreast and right in line,
Some swims fast and some swims slow
But across to the other side they go.

You must float the wagon with driftwood logs
And land it across where there ain't no bog.
They drag it across to the other side
With saddles and pack ropes spliced and tied.
It had to be done because the boss
He done give powders to swim across.

That Letter

I rode to that box a settin' on a post beside the trail,
That our outfit used fur gettin' all their messages and mail.
There I got a little letter and the envelope was pink,
It shore set me feelin' better but it soter made me think.
Yes the feelin' was surprisin' onderneath my Stetson hat.
I could feel my hair a risin' like the bristles of a cat.

Well I tore the letter open and I read it through and through.
All the time I was a hopin' I would savvy what to do.
Men is quick upon the trigger, comes to tangle ups and fights,
But a woman, you caint figger what she means by what she writes.
It was purty and invitin' like a sunny day in spring,
She had done a heap of writin' but she hadn't said a thing.

Now, when men folks start to writin' you can mostly onderstand,
And the stuff that they're a sightin' stands out plain jest like a brand
They don't never do no playin' they've a sort of sudden way,
For they start right in by sayin' what they started out to say.
Men is given to expressin' what they mean, right then and there,
But a woman keeps you guessin' till your mind goes everywhere.

Fer a spell I'd do some thinkin' then I'd start agin and read;
I kept frownin' and a blinkin' till at last I got her lead.
In that letter there was lurkin' jest one simple plain idee.
When I got my mind a workin' it was plain enough to see.
Fer she said her and her mother, come a Saturday next week
Would be over with her brother to the dance on Turkey Creek.

On the start, you see, I never had no notice what she meant.
She had fixed it up right clever in the way the letter went.
Man! I shore did whoop and beller when the idee hit me fair.
She would come without no feller and she aimed to meet me there.
It shore made me like her better fer that bashful gal of mine,
Went and built that whole durned letter, jest to write that single line.

That Little Blue Roan

Most all of you boys have rode hosses' like that;
He wasn't too thin and he never got fat,
His ears always up; he had bright wicked eyes
And don't you forgit he was plenty cow wise.

The old breed that had a moustache on his lip
He was high at the wethers and low at the hip,
His head and his fets and his pasters was black,
And a stripe of the same run the len'th of his back.

Cold mornin's he'd buck and he all us would kick;
No hoss for a kid or a man that was sick.
But Lord what a bundle of muscle and bone,
A hoss for a cowboy that little blue roan.

For an after noon hoss for workin' the herd,
He could turn any thing but a lizzard or bird.
He could pull a rope and the way he could squat:
'He could hold any critter when once he got sot.

And for ropin' outside? How that hoss could move out,
He was to 'em before they knowed what 'twas about,
And runnin' down hill didn't faize him aytall.
He was like a buck goat and he never did fall.

One day in the foothills he gave me a break.
He saved me from makin' an awful mistake.
I was ridin along at a show, easy pace.
Takin' stock of the cattle that grazed in that place.

When I spied a big heifer without any brand.
How the boys ever missed her I don't understand;
For none of the stock in that country was wild.
It was like takin' candy away from a child.

She never knowed just what I had on my mind.
'Til I bedded her down at the end of my twine,
And wropped her toes up in my old hoggin' string
And was buildin' a fire to heat up my ring.\

I figgered, you see, I was there all
alone, 'Til I happened to glance at that little blue roan.
He seemed to be usin' his nostrils and ears,
And I knowed right away there was somebody near.

Instead of my brand, well, I run on another,
I used the same brand that was on the calfs mother.
For my hoss he was watchin' a bunch of pinon,
And I shore took a hint from that little blue roan.

I ontied her feet, pulled her up by the tail,
With a kick on the rump for to make the calf sail.
I had branded her proper and marked both her ears
When out of the pinons two cow men appears.

They both turned the heifer and got a good look
While I wrote the brand down in my old tally book,
There was nothin' to do so they rode up and spoke,
And we all three set down for a sociable smoke.

The one owned the critter I'd happened to brand.
He told me his name and we grinned and shook hands.
Which he mightn't have done if he only had known,
The warn in' I got from that little blue roan.

That Smoke

Have you noticed a man with his pots and his pans
A tryin' to cook on the ground
And it ain't any joke the way that the smoke
Will foller that feller around.

If the man crouches down it goes close to the ground
And he can't see the stuff in his pan
If he raises up high it goes right in his eye
And mighty near blinds the pore man.

He gits his pot hook fer to take a good look
At the biscuits he's tryin' to bake.
But right then he can't see where the lid ort to be
And he dassen't to make a mistake.

Yes down through the years comes the memory of tears
And of grub that was scorched or half raw
How the camp fire smoked and you blinded and choked
Just to get a few bites in your craw.

Them Store Clothes

Do you remember the clothes that you wore?
Them you got at the old general merchandise store.
You had sent off fer boots and you had a good hat.
But yore tailor made outfit was finished with that.

Them cheap onder drawers. Even now you must laff
How you wropped 'em around with a once and a half.
You was jest a slim kid, but you belted 'em in,
With a piece of stick whittled sharp fer a pin.

Them cheap heavy socks. No they caint be forgotten.
Three sizes too big. Some was wool, some was cotton.
Another fine thing was that long ondershirt.
When you set in the saddle it nacherly hurt.

Fer ease and fer comfort there wasn't much chance,
With the tail wadded up in the seat of yore pants.
But the warm flannel shirt, either gray or dark blue,
Was a comfort at least, give the Devil his due.

I guess almost every old cow boy recalls
Our friend Levi P. Strauss, and his blue overalls
A new pair onderneath and an old pair on top.
So dirty they'd stand up alone and not drop.

The old duckin' coats with the corderoy collars,
And the cheap blanket linin', cost three or four dollars.
A cotton bandanna tied loose 'round yore neck,
Seemed to soter belong, and completed the wreck.

Yes, the ways and the times and the people is changed.
Now the folks and their clothin' are better arranged.
But I bet you remember the clothes that you wore.
Them you got at the old general merchandise store.

They Can Take It

Yes, it's just a bunch of hosses standin' out there in the rain.
The reason they are doin' it is easy to explain.
There is no shelter handy, so to travel ain't no good.
And they wouln't go into a barn, not even if they could.

It is just a little weather, and they're plenty used to that.
Like a cow boy in the open, livin' onderneath his hat.
All the hosses and the people that has lived their life outside,
Seems to have a constitution that can take it on the hide.

Without a bit of thinkin' I could tell you right from here,
Of hosses livin' on the range as long as thirty year.
While the hosses that's in stables, and was always roofed and fed;
Lots of them before they're twenty, has been hauled off plenty dead.

So it seems the way with people, and it seems the way with stock,
And the cedar grows the toughest when it's right amongst the rocks.
That's why hosses, men and women, if they're made of proper stuff,
Gits along a whole lot better if they're raised a little rough.

Thinkin'

It's an easy job herdin' "Parada."
Yore old hoss is standin' close by.
You are watchin' the drift of the shadders
that's made by the clowds in the sky.
There's a breeze blowin' over the mesa.
It pulls at the brim of yore hat.
You feel soter careless and lazy,
but it sets you to thinkin' at that.

Of the towns where the folk herd together
with sidewalks and plenty of light.
They are sheltered and out of the weather,
they sleep in a house every night.
There's plenty of good drinkin' water
and places to eat night and day.
They live like a man really oughter,
you wish you was livin' that way.

You know lots of outfits and bosses,
but that's jest a cow puncher's chance.
You begin when you're young wranglin' hosses,
and wind up a cook at some ranch.
You figger it's really a pity.
You've been on the range since a kid.
You would shore like to go to the City,
but what could you do if you did?

Your idees get twisted and broken.
You reach for your papers and sack.
You reckon you'll do some more smokin',
you turn with the wind to your back.
How things will work out there's no knowin'
but the cattle are startin' to stray,
So you'd better git up and be goin'
fer thinkin' don't help anyway.

The Time To Decide

Did you ever stand on the ledges,
On the brink of the great plateau,
And look from their jagged edges
On the country that lay below?

When your vision met no resistance
And nothing to stop your gaze,
Till the mountain peaks in the distance
Stood wrapped in a purple haze.

On the winding water courses
And the trails on the mountain sides,
Where you guided your patient horses
On your long and lonesome rides.

When you saw Earth's open pages,
And you seemed to understand
As you gazed on the work of ages,
Rugged and rough, but grand,

There-the things that you considered strongest
And the things that you thought were great,
And for which you had striven longest,
Seemed to carry but little weight.

While the things that were always nearer
The things that you thought were Small
Seemed to stand out grander and clearer,
As you looked from the mountain wall.

While you're gazing on such a vision,
And your outlook is clear and wide,
If you have to make a decision,
That's the time and place to decide.

Although you return to the city
And mingle again with the throng;
Though you should be softened by pity,
Or bitter from strife and wrong.

Though others should laugh in derision,
And the voice of the past grow dim;
Yet, stick to the cool decision
That you made it on the mountain's rim.

To Those Who Have Gone Before

They were comrades in hours of gladness,
They were friends in the hours of need.
They were close at our side in the blizzard,
They have battled the mad stampede.

No monument tells their story.
No word from a poet's pen.
But they carved the scrolls to their memory,
In the hearts and the lives of men.

Their faces gleam in the embers,
As we rest in some far out camp;
Alone with the voices of the night wind,
And the picketed horse's tramp.

We thank the All Wise Creator
That we met with them here on Earth.
Those characters bold and daring,
But strong in their sterling worth.

For regardless of Fame or Fortune,
We know when our lives are through;
We will meet with the God who made us,
And the souls of the friends we knew.

The Troop Hoss

No more does the cavalry form in its ranks
With its stompin' and shakin' of manes.
They ride in the "Jeeps" and they charge with the tanks
And they do all their scoutin' with planes.

The day of the cavalry hosses is done.
No longer the people will see 'em.
Like the cap and ball rifle and buffalo gun.
They are headed toward the museum.

I reckon most any old trooper enjoys
To think of the comrades he knowed,
But any old time that he thinks of the boys,
He remembers the hosses he rode.

Old cavalry hosses was smart and that's shore.
They went at their work with a will.
They knew where they belonged in the line and the "Four"
And even a rookie could drill.

He stood on his rights in formation or group.
He's a troop hoss and that's how he deals.
He claims his "Four feet from the nose to the croup";
If you crowd him look out for his heels.

How well I remember that troop hoss of mine,
A squealin' and shakin' his head,
And pawin' the dirt on the old picket line
When he knowed it was time to be fed.

Yes the troopers were tough and the hosses was rough.
Neither one educated or "Super."
But there never were friends among hosses and men,
Like the cavalry hoss and the trooper.

The Veiled Rider

It was down at the home ranch, a bunch of cow pokes
Got on an old hoss that was only half broke.
They saddled him up and they hazed him around,
But none of them rode him. They stayed on the ground.

The cook he laffed at 'em and laffed mighty hard.
Then the boys they allowed that the cook wasn't barred.
But it shore did amaze 'em to see the cook crawl
Right up in the saddle, yes apron and all.

The hoss took to buckin' all over the place.
The cook's apron flew up and covered his face.
His stirrups was long and he had to pull leather
But the cook was on top when they finished together.

One waddy he grins and remarked to the boss,
"Seems they blindfold the rider now, 'stead of the hoss."
The cook looked at the boss sorter mournful and said;
"His whole crew aint wuth seven dollars a head.

I buried my face in my apron allright,
Bit I done it to shut out the pitiful sight.
Like a bunch of fresh toad frogs that been rained down.
Them pore rannies hoppin' and yappin' around.

I will own up right now,I'm a cranky old cook,
But there's sights where really upsets me to look.
That had been out and cooked for a bunch of real hands.
And an outfit like that would disgust any man."

Warmin' One Side

It is nice for to set in a room with steam heat,
Or a stove with a fender to cock up yore feet.
With sump thin' to read, and a plenty of light,
A man feels so good he could set there all night.

But take it in winter, a ridin' the range,
A small open fire feels good for a change.
When yore tired and cold and yore hoss needs a rest
And the wind cuts right in through yore old leather vest
.
It ain't like a home, but you shore do admire
To git down on the ground by a little wood fire.
Of course you can only git warm on one side.
You are freezin' yore face while you git yore leigs fried.

But a man has one chance, for however he stands,
He can still git the warmth on his feet and his hands.
And by turnin' and twistin' and changin' about,
He shore can come mighty near gittin' thawed out.

When you git yore hoss rested and git soter warm,
You must finish yore ride in the cold and the storm.
And a feller shore savvys without bein' told,
When he sets on his saddle he'll find it right cold.

So he takes him a final good warmin' perhaps,
On the place where there ain't any seat in his chaps,
And while there's still heat in the cloth and the hide,
He is up in the saddle and ready to ride.

Was It Scare

I have heered fellers say that they never was skeered.
Well, things might have been different from what they appeared.
Now take it fer instance, some braggin' cow poke
Has to git onto a hoss that ain't broke.
His knees gits to shakin', his voice it pitched high,
And he sounds like his throat was all dusty and dry.
And he chokes at the horn till his knuckles turns white,
He is jest energetic; it couldn't be fright.

Or mebby some night when the cattle stampede
He is caught in a place where he could bend the lead,
He pulls out and widens and lets the herd go.
He didn't quit tryin', his hoss was too slow.
If yore swinimin' a herd and they start millin' 'round,
And there's plenty of chance fer a feller to drown.
He makes the excuse that he jest couldn't stay
On account of a current that washed him away.

If he happens to git in a quarrel with some one
That has three or four notches cut onto his gun,
It ain't 'cause he's skeered that he runs out of town.
He jest makes him so mad that he caint stay around.
If he gits in a fight where he hasn't a chance
And gits knocked fer a loop on the seat of his pants;
He don't jump up and run on account of a scare.
He jest took a notion to start fer some where.

I reckon the most of you know how it feels
When a rattle snake whizzes right close to yore heels.
You know mighty well that it isn't a scare
That sends you a bouncin' ten feet in the air
It's jest the idee you might make a mistake
While yore trompin' around there and hurt the pore snake.

Some times when a married man takes a few drinks
And his woman starts tellin' him all that she thinks.
It ain't 'cause he's skeert that he makes fer the door.
He's afraid she'll git hoarse if she talks anymore.
So be keerful in judgin' the way a man acts
Don't say he was skeered till you know all the facts.
And a feller jest might be misjudgin' some one
'Cause he hollered fer help and lit out on the run.

But with me, when my heart started beatin' too quick.
When I felt my knees shake and my stummick turn sick,
And my skelp started raisin' the roots of my hair,
I knowed rightaway what it was, It was scare.

Wet Boots

A cowboy goes onder a turrible strain,
When he tries to wear boots that's been soaked in the rain.
He pulls and he wiggles, and after he's tried,
He gits him some flour and sprinkles inside.

Then he gits him two jack knives; puts one in each lug,
And he stomps and he pulls till his eyes start to bug.
Next he tried a broom handle-a awful mistake.
Which same he finds out when he feels the lug break.

The toes and the heels they bust out of his socks,
And it's awful to hear how that cowpuncher talks.
He open his knife and it shore is a sin,
Fer he cuts his new boots till his feet will go in.

I reckon old timer, you know how he feels.
You have kicked bunk house walls and the chuck wagon wheels.
And you know when yore older, there's nothin' to gain
From buyin' tight boots if you work in the rain.

When A Pony Slips His Pack

When you hear a feller braggin'
that he never has been throwed,
Well, there ain't been many hosses
that the feller ever rode.
If he ever was a cowboy,
it's plum safe to bet your stack,
That he was sometimes the victim
when a pony slipped his pack.

He's been throwed right at the wagon
while the whole crew laughed and smiled.
He's been dumped out in some canon
and he walked fer several miles.
He's been throwed by tricky hosses
when they ketched him settin' slack,

Yes, a hoss can really do it
if he wants to slip his pack.
There was times that it was funny
and it didn't even hurt.
He jest sort of lit a-rollin'
when he landed in the dirt.
There was times again he thought
he felt his spinal colyum crack,
Fer he landed hard and solid
when the pony slipped his pack.

He's been bucked out of his saddle
and from onderneath his hat.
He's been throwed by vicious hosses
that has kicked him in the slats.
He's been careless with his saddle cinch
and let it git too slack.
When he felt the saddle slippin',
well, the pony shed his pack.

So, a man develops sumpthin'
    with the passin' of the years.
You could mebby call it caution
    or it might be jest plain skeer.
Fer he thinks back how he suffered
    in some bunk house or shack,
Gittin' over things that happened
    when a pony shed his pack.

When Connors Rode Rep For The Lord

One time they was givin' a big work fer souls,
They was plum over stocked so they say.
The owners all over that section was told
To come and help take 'em away.

The Devil he come and brought with him three hands
That was nearly as smart as their boss.
They was there representin' the old Pitch Fork brand
Buck Connors was there fer The Cross.

All three of them hands and the Devil was wise,
They thought they was runnin' things, but,
Buck Connors he pulled his hat down to his eyes
And rode in and started the cut.

All four of them fellers sez never a word,
They figgered they might git a break.
They watch everything that come out of the herd,
But Buck never made a mistake.

When he finished his cut he rode up to the boss
And he sez, "Well I reckon I'm through.
I got everything that belong to the Cross
And I'm turnin' it over to you."

So the throw back went home to the ranch in the sky
And the Devil he never once scored.
Not even Old Satan hisself could git by
When Buck Connors rode rep fer the Lord.

When He Cold Jaws

When yore set in the saddle and up on a hoss,
You git the idee that yore mebbyso boss.
Yore feet in the stirrups, yore hands on the rein
You feel like the Lord of the mountains and plain.
Like you run the whole country and made all the laws.
But the difference it makes when yore pony cold jaws.

You jump a few wild ones and start to turn 'em.
They try to break past and you reckon you'll learn 'em.
You raise in yore stirrups and lift fer a run,
But you haven't gone far till you see what you've done.
They race down a hill and make fer a draw,
Then yore hoss slings his head and you feel him cold jaw.

His head in the crown piece, he shore does know how.
He is after his head and he's got it right now.
You use all the stren'th in yore arms and yore shoulders.
He knocks the sparks out of the slide rocks and boulders.
A mighty sick feel in' comes into yore craw,
Fer you never did think that this hoss would cold jaw.

It ain't no use to pull. The reins tear through your grip.
He crashes through brush and you feel yore clothes rip.
About all you can do is to hang on and ride.
You feel the cold sweat breakin' out on yore hide
You had run past yore cattle the last that you saw
And yore hoss races on with an iron cold jaw.

At last he gits winded. You bend the old brute.
One sale is tore loose from the toe of yore boot.
The stock you was after, you nere will know
Which way or direction they happened to go.
You have left half yore shirt on a bunch of cat claw,
Fer it shore wrecks a hand when his hosses cold jaw.

When To Get Tough

A shy, shrinken man makes me tired;
I hate men that bluster and bluff.
The feller I always admired
Was the man that knew when to get tough.
When the boys gather in 'round the fire,
All happy and cheerful of nights;
There's none of them really admire
To hear a man tell how he fights.

But when you meet up with a feller
That never did treat you half white,
And he tells everybody you're yeller,
'Till folks get to thinkin' he's right;
You want to be quick, but be steady
Don't let him win out on a bluff.
Next time that he starts it, be ready
That's the time that you want to git tough!

If your hoss is plum gentle and older
Than, perhaps, a good cow puncher needs,
Don't spur the old brute in the shoulder,
And dig at his ribs till he bleeds.
For you know it don't take a clean sitter,
Nor a man that is awful brave,
To torture some gentle old critter
That's a-tryin' his best to behave.

But when you git up on a pony
That goes in the air and swaps ends,
And he seems to consider you phony—
Jest one of them easy-mark men;
When he goes in the air like a rocket,
When he rocks in his plunges and reels;
When you feel your legs strain in the socket,
And the spurs a'most tear from your heels,
When he's buckin' and bawlin' and screamin',

When he's knockin' you blind with his stuff –
Take to him, old boy, like a demon –
That's the time when you want to be tough.

Don't beat up the broken-down cattle
Because they can't keep in the lead.
If you're really a-Iongin' fer battle
Some night the big steers will stampede.
If you help start the leaders to millin'
You'll find you got battle enough.
Jest help keep the cattle from spillin'
That's the time for a man to get tough.

Don't set in the shade in the summer,
And tell how you used to buck snow,
'Till you put the whole crowd on the hummer,
And nobody else had a show.
But when you git caught in a blizzard,
And you feel the cold rush of its breath,
You'd better have sand in your gizzard,
You're matched in a battle with Death.
When you've crouched for perhaps twenty hours
By a fire in under a bluff
It certainly tries a man's powers–
And it's then that you want to be tough.

When calves are so little they stagger
It don't take a feller that's bright,
To treat them too rough and then swagger,
Like a man in a Spanish bull-fight.
When you rope one as big as his mother,
By a horn and a foot on one side,
And he's up and you're facin' each other
Before you can git the brute tied;
When your half broken horse goes a kitin' ,
And the bull charges in with a snuff–
If you're aimin' to practice bull-fightin'
That's the time you want to git tough.

When some fellers has opened their throttles
Some roastin' hot night in a shack;
When they've pulled the corks out of the bottles,
And you know that they won't put 'em back;
If you're feelin' real peaceful and festive,
Why, help them to swaller the stuff;
But never git peevish or restive –
It's a mighty poor time to git tough.

When late the next morning you waken
And find you fell off of your horse,
And you see that the critter has taken
A route that layout of your course;
When the sun stabs your eyes like a dagger,
When your stomach's so sick that you sway,
Your knees are so weak that you stagger,
Yet you know you must be on your way.
For the sun's getting hotter and hotter –
Mirages and dust devils dance;
You know it's eight mile to the water –
You must make it or else feed the ants.
Folks that brace up on bromo and fizzes,
They reckon they're trouble enough,
But out where the desert sun sizzles–
That's the place where you'd better be tough.

So it's no use to bluster or bristle –
It's no use to swagger or pose,
They'll learn if it's fat or hard gristle
That covers the bridge of your nose.
Fur if you keep on punchin' cattle
You'll find you've got trouble enough.
Jest hold down your job and your saddle,
And you won't have to try to be tough.

When You Buried Your Face In The Alkali Drink

This mornin' at breakfast you raised a big fuss
When you found in yore glass jest a small bit of dust
You did so much whinin', before you was through,
I had to look twicet to make shore it was you.
Come on my old pardner, remember and think
When you buried yore face in the alkali drink.

When you galloped to git there ahead of the herd
And fill yoreself up 'fore the water was stirred
You got down on all fours on yore knees and yore fists
And the mud and the slime come up over yore wrists.

Them cute little bugs so alert and alive
That come up with a shrug and went back with a dive.
You didn't care much if you swallered a few.
It would shore kill the bugs and it never hurt you.
Come on my old pardner, remember and think
When you buried yore face in the alkali drink.

It was thicker than water and thinner than pulp,
But you and the old hoss you drunk gulp for gulp.
Right up on yore cheek come the froth frum the bit.
The cattle was comin', 'twas no time to quit.
Come on my old pardner, remember and think
When you buried yore face in the alkali drink.

This mornin' you set there, so pudgy and pink,
And whined like a baby. Folks never would think
You had once been a man with a chest and a jaw,
A grin on his face and some sand in his craw.
Come on my old pardner, remember and think
When you buried yore face in the alkali drink.

What wouldn't I give jest to see you once more,
Leanin' up ginst the side of the old bunk house door.
In some battered up boots and some torn dirty clothes,
And a blowin' some cigarette smoke through yore nose.
You have been on the level, old pardner of mine.
All down through the years you have treated me fine.
I like you today, but I like best to think
Of the days when you raced with the herd for a drink.

When You're Throwed

If a feller's been a straddle
Since he's big enough to ride,
And had had to put a saddle
On just every sort of hide;
Though it's nothin' they take pride in,
Most of fellers I have knowed,
If they ever done much ridin'
has at various times got throwed.

It is when the bunch is startin'
For a round up some fine day,
That you feel a little onsartin
'Bout some little wall eyed bay.
Fer he swells to beat the nation
When you're cinchin' up the slack,
And he keeps an elevation
In your saddle at the back.

He starts rairin' and a jumpin'
And he strikes when you git near,
And you cuss 'im and you thump 'im
'Till you git 'im by the ear.
Then your right hand grabs the saddle.
And you catch your stirrup, too,
And you 'low to light astraddle
Like a wooly "Buckaroo."

But he drops his head and switches.
And he gives a backwards jump.
Out of reach your stirrup twitches.
But your right spur grabs his hump.
And, "Stay with 'im," shouts some feller.
Though you know it's hope forlorn.
Yet to show that you aint yeller
Still you choke the saddle horn.

But you feel one rein a droppin,
And you know he's got his head,
And your shirt tail's out and floppin'
An' the saddle pulls like lead.
Oh, it ain't no use a tryin'
For your spurs begin to slip
Then you're upside down and flyin'
And the horn tears from your grip.

Then you feel a vague sensation
As upon the ground you roll,
Like a violent separation
'Twixt your body and your soul.
And you land agin a hummick
Where you lay and gap fer breath,
An' there's sumpthin' grasps your stummick
Like the awful clutch of death.

You feel shaky on your trotters
When at last you try to stand,
And the landscape round you totters
And your mouth is fill of sand,
An' they swear you beat a circus
Or a "hoochy koochy" dance,
Moppin' up the canon's surface
With the busom of your pants.

Tickled plum into conniptions,
Them boys gathers in a group,
And gives various descriptions
How you looped the spiral loop.
Yes, some fellers gives perscriptions
How a broncho should be rode.
But there's few that gives descriptions
Of the times when they got throwed.

Who Told The Biggest

One night a bunch of buckaroos
Were gathered 'round a fire;
And each one wished to air his views
Before he should retire.

They talked about the world's advance,
They argued on reforms,
Until somebody, just by chance,
Began to talk of storms.

"One time," remarked old Angus Greame,
"The year I worked for Law,
In Utah, why a cloudburst came—
The worst I ever saw.

"It washed the soil all off the knobs
The boulders jumped and bounded,
And seven fellers lost their jobs
On 'count of bein' drownded.

"It rained so hard,Lord bless your souls,
That when it let up, why,
The water from the gopher holes
Rebounded six foot high."

A lank Missourian gave a shrug
And slowly shook his head.
He bit a chew from off his plug
As if he chewed on bread,

"I 'low," he said, and then he spat
A dozen feet or so,
"It rained some down where I was at
A couple years ago.

"It rained a hour, mighty hard;
It drowned our Jersey bull.
The wagon stood out in the yard,
It rained the box most full.

"It lacked of comin' to the top,
A inch, or thereabout;
I reckon 'twould have filled it up,
But I'd left the end gate out."

"I'll tell you what, the fact remains,"
We heard a deep voice say;
"Our blizzards sure beats all your rains
Back home in Ioway.

"One time a blizzard hit our town
Along in nineteen two.
The stuff that wasn't fastened down
Jest riz right up and flew.

"The roof came off the City Hall
And tumbled all 'round.
It blowed our mule again a wall
Ten feet above the ground.

"It blowed so hard that I'll declare
You couldn't git your breath;
It held that pore old mule up there
Until he starved to death."

One boy rubbed Old Johnny Baize's head
A smile upon his face.
"That's what the jackass got," he said,
"For stayin' in one place."

"That's right," replied old Johnny Baize,
"It often happens so.
I stay where I was born and raised;
I ain't no jackass though."

A boy from Arizona spoke,
"I'll tell you something strange;
It's sure the truth, and not no joke,
It happened on this range.

"I had a yellow dog called Snap;
One day I tied him up.
He opened up his mouth to gap—
A whirlwind hit that pup.

"It picked him up and turned him 'round
It spun him all about,
And left him layin' on the ground
Jest turned plum inside out."

A man from Kansas then spoke up.
"I don't exactly know
About a whirlwind and a pup—
I know how cyclones go,

"My Pa and Ma took up a claim
Along in Ninety-three.
With sister Sue and sister Mame,
And brother Bill and me.

"We built a house and barn and well—
The place did look immense.
We broke up sod fer quite a spell
And built some wire fence.

"And then one day a cyclone hit—
I heard our old cow beller;
The house went up and never lit
And left us in the cellar.

"The barn got up and danced a jig,
The wire fence broke loose.
Our little poll and chiny pig
Flew circles like a goose.

"Down came a hoss and then a boot
Close follered by a houn'.
It blowed our well plum out by root
And turned it upside down.

"My mother fainted from the scare,
So did my sister Sue;
We hadn't water there,
We couldn't bring' em to.

"Us boys we started on the run
Close followed by the houn'!
But when we got there we was done—
The well was upside down.

"I had a bucket, Bill a cup—
I don't know where we got 'em
We found the well was wrong side up—
The water in the bottom.

"We couldn't reach it if we tried,
Dad got to lookin' sadder.
My brother Bill sat down and cried;
I run to git a ladder.

"And jest as I was gittin' back
The lightnin' hit the well
Right on the bottom side ker-whack—
And blowed it all to — Well,

"That's jest about the worst cyclone
I ever chanced to see.
We used to talk of it at home;
My brother Bill and me."

"That may be so," said Old Man Carns,
"Of course I won't deny,
Some of you feelers jest told yarns,
But someone told a lie."

Winter Work

Tryin' to git the cattle in. Movin' mighty slow.
Out there in the winter wind, wadin' through the snow.
Frost nips at his ears and nose. See the way he slumps.
You can tell he's' bout half froze by the way he humps.

Winter cows don't jump and run, so you needn't worry.
Aim no use to crowd 'em none. They won't try to hurry.
Them old cows aim none too strong, got to use some reason.
Keep 'm movin', poke along, cussin' and a freezin'.

They will make it there, you hope. Take 'em quite a bit.
You can swear, don't use yore rope. If you do they'll quit.
Grouch has got old cowboy now, 'bout to git him down.
Wisht he'd never seen a cow. Wisht he was in town.

But when he gits a chance to eat, he'll begin to thaw.
Warmin' up his hands and feet, supper in his craw.
He will think the world's all right. Go to bed, and then,
He'll be up before daylight, startin' out again.

Workin' It Over

It don't matter much what a cow boy may own,
You never can git him to leave it alone.
He always has some fool idee in his head,
'Bout his saddle or pack outfit, even his bed.

Supposin' his saddle is made with square skirts,
It worries that waddy ontil his soul hurts.
He gits out his knife and he cuts the skirts round;
Then he stitches the edges, or laces 'em down.

Then, mebby he'll cut the chafes off from his cinches,
He will splice out some straps or cut off a few inches.
He will cut at his pack outfit and rip out the stitchin'
While he changes the breast rig or mebby the britchin'

He will whittle his bridle, and 'fore he gits through
He has got both his spur straps cut half way in two.
When his outfit's plum ruint he goes to the store;
He buys some new stuff and starts whittlin' once more.

The Wreck

You was chasin' that steer. He was mad, he was hot.
You built up a big loop, and you throwed and you caught.
You aimed to go past him and finish the trick,
But you made a mistake and things happened too quick.

He quit runnin' straight and dodged off to the right,
Before you could faller he had the rope tight.
He went to the end and he tore your hoss down,
But it upset the steer, they was both on the ground.

Just how you got clear you could never quite tell.
You started to jump and you reckon you fell.
But you got that tail holt and you finished the thing.
For you wrapped his toes up in yore old hoggin' string.

The hoss he was strugglin' and workin' for slack.
It might ruin that hoss if yore saddle slipped back,
You run jumped on his head and you held him down too.
And you oncinched the saddle before you were through.

You was feared he'd pull loose when he started to rise,
So you tied your neck handkercher over his eyes.
Yes, old boy, you won out by a mightly long chance.
You used most of yore outfit, 'cept mebby your pants.

You was pantin' and shakin' and all overhet.
You could taste all the bacon and coffee you'd et.
Man! you shore got a jerkin' and maulin' around,
For things gits mighty rough, when your hoss is tore down.

You Never Tell That

You are jest an old waddy that's been everywhere.
You've about held your own and done more than your share.
You wind some big windies you like mighty well,
But there's now and then things that you never do tell.

You tell of the days when you was a top hand
And you rode that wild outlaw that bucked off the brand.
But the mornin' that old wrangle mule got you down,
And he laid you out cold when you lit on the ground,
And he drove your head out through the top of your hat;
Well, somehow or other, you never tell that.

You tell of the time when you went to a dance,
And none of the other boys there had a chance.
How you wore your new clothes, and you outshined 'em all.
And you rode away home with the belle of the ball.

But the time when you travelled for over ten mile
Jest to set there and talk to some gal fer a while;
And you looked in the winder and happened to see
She was settin' in there on another boy's knee,
And you sulked and you pouted fer weeks like a brat;
You remember all right, but you never tell that.

You can tell how you won in a fist and skull fight,
But you started a scrap in a bar room one night,
and some banty weight runt knocked you blind as a bat.
Now somehow or other, you never tell that.

You can tell about gamblin'.It shore was a shame
How you pulled a fast trick and broke up a slick game.
Perhaps you remember one evenin' old pard.
You was watchin' a feller that marked the third card;
And you fell fer the trick and they busted you flat.
When you talk about gamblin', you never tell that.

Another big windy you shore like to tell.
How you got drunk in town and would holler and yell.
How you took down the street with your hoss on the run
And the people all ducked when you rolled your six gun.

But the time the town marshall, that quiet old man,
Grabbed the back of your neck and you went to the can;
And he throwed you in jail and went south with your gat,
Well somehow or other, you never tell that.

And all of them women that follered you 'round.
They jest wouldn't keep off when you once turned 'em down.
Do you ever remember one gal that you met?
You was drinkin' I know, and a little upset.

And when you got sober, you found out next day,
She had gone out of town with your whole summer's pay.
And you never discovered jest where she was at.
No, you haven't forgot, but you never tell that.

Then there was that time when a warnin' came through,
That the sheriff was out with a warrant fer you.
You went out from there jest a foggin' your tail,
And thanked God fer the snow storm that covered your trail
And you changed hosses twice 'fore you took off your hat.
And you never went back, and you never tell that.

Never mind my old pardner, in times long ago,
We all did a few things we don't want folk to know.
Most people we knowed in the days that's gone by
Acted foolish some times, so did you, so did I.

If you know some old feller that made a mistake;
Say nothin' about it and give him a break.
If you know sumpthin' bad, keep it under your hat.
Tell the best that you know, but don't ever tell that.

Your First Saddle

You never remember the school days you missed
You perhaps have forgotten the first girl you kissed
Or even forgot the first dollar you loaned,
But you'll never forget the first saddle you owned.

What matter if some one had thrown it away
How well you remember that wonderful day,
When you carefully scanned while trying to find
A few patches of wool where the skirts had been lined.

That battered old hull was the pride of your life.
How you patiently toiled with a nail and a knife.
You cut your whangs out of old bridles and chaps,
Robbed harness and saddles for leitigo straps.

And the bare iron horn; even now you must laugh
How you covered it up with a portion of calf.
Those gunny sack cinches you carefully stitched
Till they held that old hull on a pony that pitched.

There were marks where big spurs had raked over the seat.
The last desperate grabs of some punchers spurred feet,
Who attempted in vain to ride unruly brutes
And the critters had sunned both his britches and boots.

As you toiled in the dust in the shade of the shed
What wonderful visions would pass through your head.
How you'd ride that old saddle in many a land.
Tie steers and twist bronchos and be a top hand.

But you heartlessly threw that old saddle away,
Out beside the corral at headquarters, one day.
You were then drawing pay and were almost a man,
And a saddle like that wasn't fit for a hand.

But I bet it was pounced on by some other kid,
Who worked it all over the same as you did.
And you would have smiled if you only had known
How he proudly bestrode the first saddle he owned.

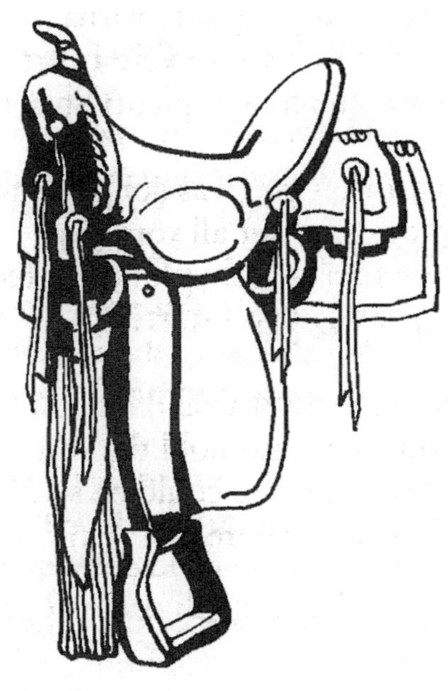

Your First Trip

Remember that first time you shipped
And went with cattle on the trip?
You asked the boss if you could go.
He said he reckoned mebbyso.

You'd been around corrals and barns
And knowed a couple dirty yarns.
You figgered out down in yore heart
That you was tough and plenty smart.

You thought that you was gone to stay
And tried to draw out all yore pay.
The boss he had you plum outsmarted
Before he even got you started.

He said he thought it would be best
To give you some and hold the rest.
He 'lowed the balance could be sent
To you, most any where you went.

Boy, when that train went down the track
You shore did rair yore hat brim back.
You felt like you could buy the Earth,
No matter what they thought 'twas worth.

Of course the train crew tried to borry.
You told 'em "No, that you was sorry."
About as near as you recall,
They stoled yore gloves, and that was all.

But once you got turned loose in town
You throwed a couple whiskies down.
Then went outside and chanced to hear
A lowd voiced pawn shop auctioneer.

I'll bet till now you ain't forgot
About that auction watch you bought.
And that there big brass ring you seen
That made yore finger all turn green.

And then you got a suit of clothes
Like they wore in minstrel shows.
With stripes as big as hitchin' straps,
And one of them there dinky caps.

And dancin' pumps with paper sales.
A neck tie like a barber pole.
And that cheap suit case made of paper,
'Twas imitation alligator.

And then you went to shootin' pool
With some pore silly talkin' fool.
You played him fer two bits a game
The way you beat him was a shame.

But he was willin' after all,
To shoot fer fifty cents a ball.
And when you got the fourth game through
He shore had put the hooks to you.

Next mornin' found you on the train
And headed back fer home again.
Where you was ridin' in the smoker,
They had a little game of poker.

You thought that you might have some luck.
That's how you lost yore last two bucks.
Back in the wash room on the train,
You put yore work clothes on again.

Yore cap and suit, and every thing.
And even to yore watch and ring,
You put in that pasteboard suit case.
You didn't want to be disgraced.

You raised the smoker winder high
And bid the whole durned works goodbye.
You throwed it out and let it lay
Somewhere along the right of way.

Fer sometime after you got back,
The boss he made a few wise cracks,
About yore suit and cap and things,
But mostly 'bout the watch and ring.

It kep you soter at a loss
To find out who had told the boss.
But now there ain't a bit of doubt.
You got the whole thing figgered out.

The boss he once made his first trip,
And, you can gamble when he shipped,
He done the same things that you did
When he was nothin' but a kid.

So that's how come the boss to know.
He done the same thing years ago.

When They've Finished Shipping Cattle In The Fall

Though you're not exactly blue,
Yet you don't feel like you do
In the winter, or the long hot summer days.
For your feelin's and the weather,
Seem to sort of go together,
And you're quiet in the dreamy autumn haze.
When the last big steer is goaded
Down the chute, and safely loaded;
And the summer crew has ceased to hit the ball;
When a feller starts a draggin'
To the home ranch with the wagon—
When they've finished shippin' cattle in the fall.

Only two men left a standin'
On the job for winter brandin',
And your pardner, he's a loafin' at your side.
With a bran-new saddle creakin',
But you never hear him speakin',
And you feel it's gain' to be a quiet ride.
But you savvy one another,
For you know him like a brother—
He is friendly, but he's quiet, that is all;
For he's thinkin' while he's draggin'
To the home ranch with the wagon—
When they've finished shippin' cattle in the fall.

And the saddle hosses stringin'
At an easy walk a swingin'
In behind the old chuck wagon mavin' slow.
They are weary gaunt and jaded
With the mud and brush they've waded,
And they settled down to business long ago.
Not a hoss is feel in' sporty,
Not a hoss is actin' snorty;

In the spring the brutes was full of buck and bawl;
But they're gentle, when they're draggin'
To the home ranch with the wagon –
When they've finished shippin' cattle in the fall.

And the cook leads the retreat
Perched high upon his wagon seat,
With his hat pulled 'way down furr'wd on his head.
Used to make that old team hustle,
Now he hardly moves a muscle,
And a feller might imagine he was dead,
'Cept his old cob pipe is smokin'
As he lets his team go pokin',
Hittin' all the humps and hollers in the road.
No the cook has not been drinkin' –
He's just settin' there and thinkin'
'Bout the places and the people that he knowed
And you watch the dust a trailin'
And two little clouds a sailin',
And a big mirage like lakes and timber tall.
And you're lonesome when you're draggin'
To the home ranch with the wagon –
When they've finished shippin' cattle in the fall.

When you make the camp that night,
Though the fire is burnin' bright,
Yet nobody seems to have a lot to say.
In the spring you sung and hollered,
Now you git your supper swallered
And you crawl into your blankets right away.
Then you watch the stars a shinin'
Up there in the soft blue linin'
And you sniff the frosty night air clear and cool.
You can hear the night hoss shiftin'
As your memory starts a driftin'
To the little village where you went to school.
With its narrow gravel streets
And the kids you used to meet,
And the common where you used to play baseball.

Now you're far away and draggin'
To the home ranch with the wagon
For they've finished shippin' cattle in the fall.

And your school-boy sweetheart too,
With her eyes of honest blue –
Best performer in the old home talent show.
You were nothin' but a kid
But you liked her, sure you did–
Lord! And that was over thirty years ago.
Then your memory starts to roam
From Old Mexico to Nome.
From the Rio Grande to the Powder River,
Of the things you seen and done –
Some of them was lots of fun
And a lot of other things they make you shiver.
'Bout that boy by name of Reid
That was killed in a stampede–
'Twas away up north, you helped 'em dig his grave,
And your old friend Jim the boss
That got tangled with a hoss,
And the fellers couldn't reach in time to save.

You was there when Ed got his'n –
Boy that killed him's still in prison,
And old Lucky George, he's is rich and livin' high.
Poor old Tom, he come off worst,
Got his leg broke, died of thirst
Lord but that must be an awful way to die.

Then them winters at the ranches,
And the old time country dances–
Everybody there was sociable and gay.
Used to lead 'em down the middle
Jest a prancin' to the fiddle–
Never thought of goin' home till the break of day.

No! there ain't no chance for sleepin'
For the memories come a creepin'
And sometimes you think you hear the voices call;
When a feller starts a draggin'
To the home ranch with the wagon –
When they've finished shippin' cattle in the fall.